Unveiling The Mysteries of
GOD'S SILENCE

SAMUEL SOWAH

FOREWORD BY DR DEBORAH ANNE BARTLETT

Unveiling The Mysteries of GOD'S SILENCE

Exploring the Voice of God in Moments of His Quietude

Unveiling The Mysteries of
GOD'S
SILENCE

Exploring the Voice of God in Moments of His Quietude

PNEUMALIFE PUBLISHING

Pneuma Life Publishing books are available at discounted prices for bulk purchase for fund-raising, premiums, sales promotions.

For details, email your request to **sales@pneumalife.com** or write us at **Pneuma Life Publishing, 12138 Central Ave, Suite 251, Mitchellville, MD 20721**

Unveiling the Mysteries of God's Silence:
Exploring the Voice of God in Moments of His Quietude

Copyright © 2024 by Samuel Sowah
samuelsowahministriesintl@gmail.com

All rights reserved. No part of this book may be reproduced in any form without permission in writing from the publisher, except in the case of brief quotations embodied in critical articles or reviews. Except otherwise indicated, all Bible quotations were taken from the New King James Version of the Bible.

Published by Pneuma Life Publishing
12138 Central Ave, Suite 251,
Mitchellville, MD 20721
www.pneumalife.com

All Rights Reserved
Printed in the United States of America
ISBN 978-1-56229-882-1

Table of Contents

Dedication	X
Acknowledgements	X
Foreword	XII
Introduction	XIV
Chapter 1. Exploring The Voice of God.	1
Chapter 2. The Deep Voice of God's Quietude.	27
Chapter 3. God Breaks the Silence.	43
Chapter 4. The Purpose of God's Silence.	61
Chapter 5. Biblical Players - Part I.	75

CHAPTER 6.
BIBLICAL PLAYERS - PART II.   89

CHAPTER 7.
THE SIGNIFICANCE OF GOD'S SILENCE.   109

CHAPTER 8.
THE TRANSFORMATIVE POWER OF
DIVINE REVELATION.   121

CHAPTER 9.
OBEDIENCE AND YIELDEDNESS TO
GOD'S WILL.   137

CHAPTER 10.
THE AFTERMATH OF GOD'S SILENCE.   153

Dedication

I dedicate this flying scroll to the manifestation of God's glory on earth, to all kingdom heroes fatigued by the numerous challenges of life for fresh strength and grace. To WPC(GPF) awaiting emergence. Finally, to Kingdom Action Ministries and the Apostolic Gatherings for global impact.

Acknowledgement

I would like to express my heartfelt gratitude to all those who contributed to make this dream come true.

First and foremost, my appreciation goes to the most Holy One for releasing this scroll to earth by my hand;
and to my wife Beverly for her unwavering support and sacrifices to see the product of this project.

I also extend my sincere appreciation to Barrister Emeka Nwankpa, Chairman of the African House of Prayer, Nairobi, Kenya; Apostle Joshua Selman, Eternity Network, Abuja, Nigeria; Bishop Dr. Emma Isong, Calabar, Nigeria; Bishop Dr. J.G. Bart-Plange, Teshie Nungua Estates, Accra, Ghana; Apostle Dr. James Obeng, Chairman network of intercessors Accra, Ghana; Lady Tonia Smith, Grace Government Services Alabama, USA; Dr. Deborah Anne Bartlett, CEO of The Economic Emancipation Movement Nassau, Bahamas; and

Bishop Dr. Joseph Nyarko Antwi, Head of Prayer, ACI Accra, Ghana. Your distant coaching and input have been instrumental in shaping this manuscript.

I am grateful to the team at Pneuma Life Publishing, especially Mr Derwin Stewarts, for their professionalism and dedication in bringing this project to fruition. Your insights and feedback have greatly enhanced the quality of this book.

I also wish to thank my brother Apostle Dr Emmanuel Gyan for his enormous input and Bishop Dr Kibby Otoo for the support along the way. Your words of encouragement kept me motivated during the challenging times.

Thank you to everyone who has played a part in this endeavour. Your contributions have made this book possible.

Foreword

Unveiling the Mysteries of God's Silence" by Samuel Sowah is a remarkable work that delves into the profound realms of God's quietude, offering invaluable insights and spiritual guidance for all those navigating the purposeful silent seasons of life.

In "Exploring The Voice of God," Samuel lays a solid foundation by breaking down the diverse ways in which God communicates with us, providing a comprehensive understanding for the journey ahead.

"The Deep Voice of God's Silence" penetrates the heart of God's quietude, revealing the hidden treasures that lie within moments of apparent stillness. The author invites readers to embrace these moments as pathways to deepen the various dimensions of intimacy with God.

Through captivating narratives in "God Breaking the Silence," Samuel demonstrates how God's intervention during periods of silence led to miraculous outcomes, showcasing His sovereignty and character.

"Biblical Players-Part I & II" serve as powerful examples, offering valuable lessons from the life experiences of faithful figures. Readers are guided through their experiences of resilience, unwavering faith, and transformation in the face of God's silence.

"The Significance of God's Silence" sheds light on the transformative power of these periods, portraying them as refining fires that shape our character, strengthen our faith, and draw us closer to God's heart.

In "Obedience and Yieldedness to God's Will," Samuel emphasises the importance of vulnerability and surrender during times of silence, encouraging readers to embrace these virtues as avenues for spiritual growth and the fulfilment of God's plan for our lives.

"The Aftermath of God's Silence" reveals that silent seasons are not empty voids to be feared but rather spheres of encounter, where faith is renewed, understanding deepens, and the presence of God is keenly felt.

Through profound insights and biblical wisdom, "Unveiling the Mysteries of God's Silence" stands as a beacon of hope and guidance for all those seeking comfort and understanding amidst life's quietude. Samuel Sowah's work assures us that God's presence is ever present, His love unwavering, and His purpose unfolding, even in the midst of silence.

This book is a powerful testament to the transformative power of embracing God's silence, guiding readers on a journey of revelation, faith, and a deeper walk with the Almighty God.

DR DEBORAH ANNE BARTLETT,
Founder/ CEO
Bartlett Communications
& The Economic Emancipation Movement
Nassau, Bahamas.

Introduction

During our earthly pilgrimage, we encounter various seasons of life, each with its own set of challenges and experiences. One such season is the window of God's silence, which stands out as the subject and heart of this book. It is a deliberate season positioned within God's sovereign plan, revealing why He sometimes chooses not to speak directly or intervene in human affairs. This serves as a signal, calling our attention to the different aspects of His interactions, whether with the earth, humanity, or satanic activities.

Traversing these moments is a significant part of our human experience. Therefore, my assignment is to call all and sundry to grasp the work being accomplished behind the scenes.

In Revelation 8:1-3, we glimpse a significant moment in John's vision of heaven, where the Lamb of God breaks the seventh seal and ushers in a window of silence in heaven. This divine interlude signifies a profound moment preceding the unfolding of subsequent events.

Driven by God's predetermined agenda within His sovereign plan, His quietude holds immense significance across different aspects of life. During this period, multifaceted workings unfold—shaping our character, dealing with satanic agendas, and positioning us strategically for destiny, accomplishing His sovereign plan.

As we go through the season, we grapple with serious complications of both spoken and unspoken interactions with God, traversing the mysteries captured within His voice and the deep silences that resonate through the overall experience.

This unfolds in the various chapters of the book, each shedding light on a facet of the subject of our focus. We begin by excavating the mystery behind God's voice, unravelling the revelations and utterances that reverberate through the experience of faith. We then traverse the veiled arena of 'God's Silence,' seeking to understand the spiritual significance of moments when He seems hidden, distant, or disconnected.

Our journey continues through the transformative phase where the window of quietude closes, giving way to the resumption of divine revelations. Understanding the purpose and significance of this period becomes crucial as we ponder the intentions behind the season.

Turning the pages of scripture, we discover players who offer insights into how God's silence and utterances have shaped their lives as individuals, families, and even nations.

The journey deepens as we explore and unpack historical and contemporary experiences, drawing connections between biblical narratives and real-life experiences of people over generations.

As we delve into the experiences of biblical figures, we uncover their wisdom, strength, and weaknesses during times of perceived disconnect from God. Ultimately, we conclude by grasping the enduring impact and transformative results that resonate in the lives of those who walked these paths.

Come with me on this insightful expedition through the chapters of the book, with each page unveiling dimensions of insight into the mysteries behind God's voice. Let's ponder the wonder between the 'spoken word' and the 'deep voice of God's silence.'

Chapter 1

Exploring The Voice of God

OD, who at sundry times and in various ways, spoke in time past to the fathers by the prophets, has in these last days spoken to us by His Son, whom He has appointed heir of all things, through whom also He made the worlds. *Hebrews 1:1-2.*

In time past, God spoke to the fathers through the prophets. These prophets were mortals chosen, inspired and anointed by God to convey His intent to those unto whom they were sent. God's voice through prophetic vessels is still relevant today.

However, in these last days scripture declares, "He speaks to us directly through His Son, Jesus Christ, who is the ultimate revelation of God himself to humanity.

Knowing God speaks is one thing; understanding how he speaks and what He communicates is a different thing altogether. This helps us to know what's on His mind, understand His character, and ways. Throughout history, God spoke to individuals and groups through diverse means and in various ways.

Let's Explore Biblical Platforms on which God speaks.

General Revelation

The concept of general revelation refers to hearing the voice of God through creation and the human conscience. His voice is made available to all regardless of cultural or religious background and can be heard and seen through natural phenomena, beauty in nature, and the complexity of the world. This points us to understanding the existence of God and His attributes.

Special or Specific Revelation

The concept of special or specific revelation refers to the voice of God uttered directly to individuals or groups through specific ways such as: The ten commandments, prophecies, divine promises, and principles.

Special revelation, as it were, offers profound insight into God's character, his plan for salvation, and guidance for righteous living.

Progressive Revelation.

The concept of progressive revelation explains, God's voice and revelation to humanity develop gradually over time, unfolding in various stages throughout history, each building on the previous revelation, providing deeper insight into God's will and character. Let it be known that the ultimate manifestation of progressive revelation is Jesus Christ, who is the manifestation of the fullness of the Godhead bodily.

The Old Testament

God's revelation to humanity was line upon line, a little here, a little there through individuals like Adam, Noah, Abraham, and Moses. He spoke through visions, dreams, and direct encounters. The giving of the law to Moses, the writings of the prophets, and the experiences of the children of Israel further expanded His revelation.

The New Testament

The ultimate of progressive revelation is Jesus Christ, the "Word made flesh". Expounded through His person, ways, teachings and works. The apostles expanded further Jesus' significance, voiced through their epistles in the New Testament.

Revelation

The final book of the Bible offers us a glimpse of God's ultimate plan for humanity and the total dominion of His Christ.

The Incarnation

Jesus Christ, the express image and ultimate revelation of God the Father. He is the fullness of the Godhead bodily Colossians 2:9, meaning, Jesus the Son of God, is the ultimate revelation of God's person and attributes to us.

The Voice of Prophetic Messengers

Throughout history, God tasked His messengers with His intent wrapped up in words. Here are some key points about the voice of prophetic messengers throughout history.

Purpose:

These messengers, not limited to the prophetic office, were instruments through whom God conveyed His intents.

Guidance:

God's messages came as instructions for righteous living, warnings of impending disasters, and guidance on moral and ethical behaviour.

Shaping History:

Their ministries and messages played a significant role in shaping the course of history, advancing God's economy on earth.

God's Non-Verbal Voice:

The concept of God's non-verbal communication refers to God speaking by way of sign language such as, symbols, prophetic acts, and types, etc.

Examples of God's non-verbal Voice in scripture:

The Burning Bush Scenario in Exodus 3.

When God appeared to Moses in the burning bush, it was a non-verbal voice. The bush burned but was not consumed, catching Moses' attention and leading to His encounter with God.

The Pillar of Cloud and Fire in Exodus 13.

During the Israelites' journey out of Egypt, God guided them with a pillar of cloud by day and a pillar of fire by night.

God's non-verbal voice through the pillar of cloud by day and pillar of fire by night conveyed several important messages:

The Presence of God:

The pillar of cloud and fire spoke of His presence.

Divine Guidance:

It spoke of His instructions and guidance, leading them on the way they were to go. When the pillar of cloud moved, they knew it was time to break camp and advance.

Light:

The pillar of fire provided light during the night, ensuring they could travel safely and see where they were going in the face of darkness.

Heat and Warmth:

In addition to the light, it provided warmth during the cold desert nights, offering comfort and protection from the elements.

Protection:

The pillar of cloud and fire were God's voice of protection. It provided shade from the scorching sun, shielded them from their enemies, and from the dangers of the wilderness.

The Parting of the Red Sea in Exodus 14.

God's miraculous act of parting the Red Sea for the Israelites to cross was God's non-verbal voice of His power , providence and sovereignty.

The Handwriting on the Wall in Daniel 5.

A mysterious hand appeared and wrote on the wall during King Belshazzar's feast, predicting the downfall of Babylon. This was God's non-verbal voice of judgement.

During His earthly ministry.

Jesus communicated in various ways, both verbally and non verbally through actions, body language, and even moments of silence. His miracles and healings were indeed powerful non-verbal displays of God's compassion, power, and the manifestation of His Kingdom.

His Healings and Miracles:

Jesus performed numerous healings, such as curing the sick, restoring sight to the blind, enabling the deaf to hear, the dumb to speak, and freeing those possessed by demons and many others. These were all acts of God's voice of kindness.

Compassion and Love:

"Jesus' miracles were divine communications of deep compassion and love for the people he healed. He touched, spoke comforting words, and showed genuine care for their well-being."

Revealing God's Kingdom:

These were signs pointing to the manifestation of God's Kingdom on earth, demonstrating His power over nature, Satan and his activities, sickness and disease signaling the dawn of a new era of God's rule and restoration.

Teaching through Actions:

Jesus taught through actions, illustrating important spiritual truths. For example, His feeding of the 5,000 highlighted the abundance of God's provision, while walking on water showed His authority over the forces of nature.

Symbolic Actions:

Jesus used symbolic actions to convey deep spiritual truth. For instance, washing his disciples' feet was a powerful demonstration of humility and service.

Moments of Silence.

During His trial before Pontius Pilate, His silence demonstrated submission to God's will and trust in His faithfulness.

In the poignant account of the woman caught in adultery (John 8:1-11), Jesus's non-verbal communication speaks volumes:

Calming Authority and Wisdom: Jesus stooped down and wrote on the ground with his finger, a gesture that exuded with absolute authority and wisdom.

Mercy and Compassion: When Jesus finally spoke, he offered mercy to the woman and challenged the hypocrisy of her accusers. His words, "He who is without sin among you, let him throw a stone at her first," echoed with compassion, showing his willingness to forgive and extend grace.

Empathy and Hope: Through his non-verbal cues, Jesus likely conveyed empathy towards the woman, who faced fear and shame. His demeanor would have communicated acceptance and understanding, offering her hope and forgiveness, despite her past mistakes.

In this profound encounter, Jesus's non-verbal communication showcased his divine attributes of wisdom, mercy, and empathy, leaving a lasting impact on both the woman and her accusers.

Through His diverse ways of communicating, Jesus revealed the heart of God to humanity, calling them to experience His love, mercy, and transformative power. Each act in moments of silence conveyed a powerful message of God's presence and the manifestation of His Kingdom.

Hearkening unto God's Voice:

Understanding what God communicates is an essential and fundamental requirement for a deeper relationship with Him, knowing His thoughts and pursuits.

Here are key components to consider as we seek to excavate, explore, and unveil God's voice:

Isaiah 30:29-30 declares:

You shall have a song
As in the night when a holy solemnity is kept,
And gladness of heart as when one goes with a flute,
To come into the mountain of the Lord,
To the Mighty One of Israel.
The Lord will cause His glorious voice to be heard,
And show the descent of His arm,
With the indignation of His anger
And the flame of a devouring fire,
With scattering, tempest, and hailstones.

Practising singing unto the Lord and keeping holy solemnity is a beautiful expression of worship that combines joyful praise with reverence and awe.

Be Joyful and Maintain a Gladsome Heart.

Therefore with joy you will draw water
From the wells of salvation. - Isaiah 12:3

Learn to defend your joy no matter the costs.

Be Thankful and Praiseful:

Psalm 95:1-2: "Oh come, let us sing to the Lord! Let us shout joyfully to the Rock of our salvation. Let us come before His presence with thanksgiving; Let us shout joyfully to Him with psalms."

Be Open and Sensitive:

Openness and sensitivity to God's voice require your choice and willingness to listen and follow divine signals.

Be Prayerful and Meditative:

Regular prayer and meditation on the word of God help us cultivate a deeper connection with God. These practices allow us to commune with Him, seek His instructions, and listen to His voice.

The Place of the gift of Discerning of Spirits:

The function of the gift of discerning spirits in one's life is crucial for distinguishing God's voice from other sources, such as our thoughts, emotions, or external influences.

Be willing to Obey Absolutely:

Responding in obedience to God's promptings is a natural outcome of a growing relationship with Him. As we learn to trust His voice and follow His leading, we experience His faithfulness and see His purposes unfold in our lives.

Ultimately, as we seek to uncover and delve into God's voice and respond obediently to His promptings and instructions, we deepen our intimacy with Him. Our relationship then transcends mere knowledge about God; it evolves into an ongoing dialogue with the living God who yearns to reveal Himself to us and lead us along life's destiny path.

THE CHANNELS THROUGH WHICH GOD SPEAKS TO US.

THE SCRIPTURES.

The scriptures convey the revelation of God's voice as a fundamental principle of our relationship with him.

"All Scripture, The Bible says', is given by inspiration of God, and is profitable for doctrine, for reproof, for correction, for instruction in righteousness, that the man of God may be complete, thoroughly equipped for every good work.

2 Timothy 3:16-17

DOCTRINE (TEACHING):

The voice of God via doctrine encompasses the core teachings of the Bible regarding God, Jesus Christ, Sin, Redemption, the kingdom of God and moral principles, aiming to bring stature and maturity to the community of believers in Christ.

Reproof (Rebuke or Convict):

God's voice through the scriptures brings conviction of sin, aligning one's life with God's will and sets the standards for living.

Correction:

God's voice through His word corrects our behaviour and informs our beliefs. It points out where we are wrong or misguided and helps us to align ourselves with God's truth and right standing.

Instruction in Righteousness:

God's voice through the scriptures instructs us in righteousness, serving as a manual for training and living. It teaches us how to cultivate virtues such as love, patience, kindness, humility, and forgiveness. Through the examples of the patriarchs, prophets, Jesus, and the apostles, we learn how to live in alignment with God's standards.

Equipping and Making Ready:

Making us ready for the Master's use involves preparing believers to be vessels fit for God's work. This readiness includes developing a deep relationship with him through prayer, studying of the word, and growing in spiritual maturity. It also involves cultivating qualities such as faithfulness, obedience, humility, and a heart of service.

God's Voice through Answered Prayer:

Jeremiah 33:3 admonishes the need to call on the Lord, and the response-promise of great and mighty things it holds. Answers to prayer reveal God's faithfulness and voice to those who call upon Him out of a pure heart and dire need.

God's Voice through His Earthly Messengers:

The prophets of old, like Isaiah, Jeremiah, and Ezekiel, served as crucial conduits for conveying God's messages to His people. They were human vessels anointed by God to articulate His voice during their time. Today, God speaks through Jesus to His church and through the church to all creation.

Diverse Ways God Speaks to Us:

His Audible Voice is the direct and intimate way he speaks, as seen in biblical accounts. For example, in Exodus 3:4, God calls Moses by name from the burning bush, initiating a dialogue which eventually led to a pivotal event in biblical history.

Ezekiel 1:3. The word of the LORD came to Ezekiel in an explicit manner, showing the personal and direct nature of God's interaction with individuals.

God's audible voice is a powerful way of His communication, showcasing His personal and direct engagement in the lives of humanity.

Dreams and Visions:

God speaks through dreams revealing His intent, offering guidance, warnings, and revelations of purpose and future events.

Biblical Examples:

Joseph's dreams of his future rulership in Genesis 37:5-11, Pharaoh's dream in Genesis 41:1-7 about the future economy of his country, Nebuchadnezzar's dream of the golden image in Daniel 2, and the visions in the book of Revelation, such as Revelation 1:1, are clear examples.

God's Heavenly Messengers:

Revelation 1:1 states: "The revelation from Jesus Christ, which God gave him to show his servants what must soon take place. He made it known by sending his angel to his servant John,"

Angels are God's heavenly messengers, who undertake diverse projects and assignments on his behalf in the earth, it's fullness, the world and its inhabitants.

Here are a few Scriptural examples:

In Luke 1:26-38. The angel Gabriel is sent to announce the birth of Jesus to Mary. Gabriel's visit to Mary was a direct result of God's command, illustrating how angels act according to God's will as messengers to the earth.

Acts 12:7-11.
In this passage, an angel helps Peter escape from prison. The angel appears to Peter, instructs him to dress and follow, and leads him out of prison, demonstrating the angels' role in aiding believers in times of need according to God's plan.

Overall, angels are seen as obedient servants of God who carry out His will, whether it's delivering messages, protecting believers, guiding individuals, or fulfilling other tasks in accordance with God's plans and purposes.

The Role of the Holy Spirit:

The Inward Witness:

The Holy Spirit provides believers with an inward witness, a deep-seated conviction or assurance of their identity as God's children. In Romans 8:16, Paul writes, "The Spirit himself bears witness with our spirit that we are God's children."

This inward witness gives believers confidence in their relationship with God and serves as a source of assurance in times of doubt or uncertainty.

Spiritual Perception:

Believers are guided by the Holy Spirit to recognize and understand spiritual truths. Spiritual perception is an atunement to the nudges, promptings and conviction of the Holy Spirit. Perception is cultivated through fasting and prayer, the study of the word, meditation and a close relationship with the Holy Spirit.

Promptings and Guidance:

The Holy Spirit speaks to the believer through inner promptings and guidance.

These promptings manifest as strong convictions about a course of action, a deep sense of peace regarding a decision, or clarity of mind when seeking God's will.

In John 16:13, Jesus promises that the Spirit will guide believers into all truth. The Holy Spirit leads believers along the right path, helping them make decisions aligned with God's will.

Discerning God's Will.

Discernment is the process of recognizing and knowing God's will in various situations.

The Holy Spirit plays a crucial role in this process by illuminating Scripture, providing wisdom, and guiding the believers' thoughts and decisions.

Romans 12:2 encourages believers to "be transformed by the renewing of the mind, to help discern what is that good, acceptable and perfect will of God."

Through the Holy Spirit's guidance, believers can discern God's will and make choices that honour Him.

God's Voice through Situations, Circumstances, and Events.

The voice of God echoes through situations, circumstances, and events in the life of the believer. Take a closer look.

Divine Providence.

Romans 8:28: God works all things together for the good of those who love Him. He orchestrates every detail of one's life to accomplish His purposes, even in face of challenging situations.

Biblical Examples.

Joseph's narrative in Genesis 50:20 depicts how God can use a difficult situation to fulfill His plan for Joseph's family.

Throughout scripture, God's providential care and sovereign control are evident in the lives of people.

The Inner Voice of the Conscience.

The human conscience serves as a significant channel through which God communicates with humanity. Here's its significance.

Role of the Conscience.

It serves as an internal moral compass, guiding individuals and aligning them with ethical and spiritual values.

The conscience convicts individuals when they violate moral or spiritual principles, prompting repentance and seeking forgiveness.

Guides Ethical Decisions.

The conscience helps individuals make ethical decisions and navigate moral dilemmas. It encourages one to consider the implications of actions, promoting paths that honour God and benefit others.

Alignment with God's Will.

The conscience prompts individuals to live in accordance with God's laws and principles.

It fosters a life of obedience, integrity, and holiness in alignment with God's purposes.

Seeker of The Truth.

The conscience is sensitive to spiritual truths and bears witness to God's moral and spiritual values.

It guides individuals in their spiritual journey, prompting them to seek truth, wisdom, and righteousness.

Development of Virtues.

By listening to and obeying the promptings and vibrations of the conscience, individuals cultivate virtues such as honesty, humility, compassion, and love.

These virtues reflect the likeness of Christ and contribute immensely to personal growth and the well-being of others.

God's Voice through Miracles, Signs, and Wonders.

Miracles, signs, and wonders are God's statements of divine purposes.

Miracles:

Miracles are extraordinary events or actions that manifest God's power, presence, and purpose. They are a demonstration of God's sovereignty over the natural course of events.

They reveal God's authority and ability to intervene in the course of human affairs.

Signs:

Signs are events, occurrences, or phenomena that carry a symbolic or meaningful message. Signs are often used by God to communicate His will, reveal His presence, and guide His people.

Signs communicate instructions, warnings, or promises from God to His people. Signs can be visual, auditory, or experiential in nature, often using the language of symbolism to convey deeper truths. They reveal aspects of God's nature, character, and purposes.

Wonders:

Wonders are extraordinary events or phenomena that evoke awe, wonder, or amazement due to their supernatural nature.

They go beyond natural explanations and inspire reverence for God, demonstrating His power, majesty, and glory.

Examples and Significance:

The Manifestation of God's Power:

Miracles, signs, and wonders depict God's power over creation and His ability to intervene in human affairs.

Examples include the parting of the Red Sea, healings by Jesus, and the outpouring of the Holy Spirit at Pentecost.

The Confirmation of God's Word.

These acts follow the voice of God's word, confirming His truthfulness and authority.

Miracles authenticate the message of God's messengers, providing compelling evidence of His presence and power.

Expression of God's Compassion.

Throughout the Gospels, we see Jesus performing miracles out of compassion for the sick, oppressed, and marginalised.

His miracles demonstrate God's desire to alleviate suffering and bring healing and restoration.

As a Witness to Unbelievers.

Miracles serve as a powerful witness to unbelievers, compelling them to acknowledge the reality of God's existence and power.

Manifestation of God's Kingdom:

Miracles, signs, and wonders reveal the reality of God's rule and reign in the world.

Jesus' ministry was characterised by the proclamation of the kingdom of God and the demonstration of its power through signs and wonders.

Expression of God's Intent.

Miracles, signs, and wonders demonstrate God's power, confirm His word, express His compassion, bear witness to unbelievers, and manifest the presence of His kingdom.

Believers are invited to recognize God's activity in their midst and respond with faith, gratitude, and obedience.

God's Voice through Divine Correction and Discipline:

God's correction and discipline are significant aspects of His voice to humanity, as depicted throughout scripture.

Scriptural Examples:

Both instances highlight God's corrective measures when His people deviate from His ways. In the Old Testament, God disciplined the Israelites through various trials like exile, defeat in war, and famine when they strayed from His path. Similarly, in the New Testament, Jesus rebuked His disciples when they misunderstood His teachings or demonstrated a lack of faith. These examples emphasize the importance of obedience and faithfulness in maintaining a relationship with God.

Purpose and Forms of Correction:

God's correction aims at bringing His people back to the right path and restoring their relationship with Him.

It also serves as an instruction, teaching believers to walk in obedience and righteousness.

Response to Correction:

A humble acceptance of wrongdoing and repentance leads to the restoration of fellowship with God.

Persistence in rebellion or disobedience may lead to escalating consequences until repentance occurs.

The Role of the Church:

The church is God's rod of discipline by holding believers accountable, confronting sin in love, and providing support and guidance.

This aligns with Jesus' instructions in Matthew 18:15-17 on how to address sin within the community of believers.

These platforms illustrate God's diverse ways of communicating with humanity, using the Scriptures as a guiding canon.

Highlights.

God's voice throughout History.

God spoke to the fathers through prophets.
The voice of prophetic vessels is still relevant today.
In these last days, he speaks to us through His Son, Jesus Christ.

Ways to Know and decipher God's Voice:

General Revelation:

Through creation and the human conscience.

Special or Specific Revelation: Direct messages like the ten commandments, prophecies, promises, principles, and miracles.

Progressive Revelation: God's unfolding revelation through history, culminating in Jesus Christ.

Progressive Revelation:

The Old Testament:

God's gradual revelation through individuals and experiences.

The New Testament:

The ultimate revelation in Jesus Christ, the teachings of the apostles.

The Book of Revelation:

A glimpse of God's ultimate plan for humanity.

The Incarnation:

Jesus Christ as the ultimate revelation of God to humanity.

Voice of Prophetic Messengers:

Purpose:

Instruments through whom God speaks His intent.

Guidance:

Instructions, warnings, and moral guidance.

Shaping History:

Messages that impact the course of events.

God's Non-Verbal Voice:

Signs and symbols used to communicate God's thoughts and ways. Examples like the burning bush, pillar of cloud and fire, parting of the Red Sea, and handwriting on the wall.

Jesus' Communicates.

Through actions, miracles, teachings, symbolic acts, moments of silence.

Revealing God's Kingdom and illustrating spiritual truths.

Hearkening unto God's Voice:

Openness, sensitivity, prayer, meditation, discernment, and obedience.

God's Voice through Various Channels.

The Scriptures:

Doctrine, reproof, correction, instruction, equipping.

Answered Prayer:

Revealing God's faithfulness.

Earthly Messengers:

Prophets as vessels of God's voice. Diverse Ways God Speaks: Audible voice, dreams, visions, heavenly messengers.

The Role of the Holy Spirit:

Believers are guided by the Holy Spirit to recognize and understand spiritual truths. Spiritual perception is an atunement to the nudges, promptings and conviction of the Holy Spirit. Perception is cultivated through fasting and prayer, the study of the word, meditation and a close relationship with the Holy Spirit.

God's Voice through Situations, Circumstances, and Events:

Divine Providence, biblical examples of God's control over circumstances.

The Inner Voice of the Conscience.

Role as a moral compass, guide to ethical decisions, alignment with God's will.

God's Voice through Miracles, Signs, and Wonders. Manifestation of God's power, confirmation of His word, expression of compassion.

God's Voice through Divine Correction and Discipline. Purpose, forms, responses to God's correction and discipline.

Platforms on which God speaks.

God's diverse ways of communicating, using the Scriptures as a guiding canon.

Chapter 2

The Deep Voice of God's Quietude

Before delving into the exploration and uncovering of the Mysteries behind God's Silence, let's first understand the meanings of the terminologies used.

Mystery:

The idea of mystery denotes something that is challenging to comprehend or elucidate. It frequently entails elements that are concealed, enigmatic, or not readily understandable by human rationale or knowledge.

In theological or philosophical contexts, a mystery alludes to a truth that surpasses human comprehension. It may involve divine truths or spiritual realities that transcend the boundaries of human understanding or logical explanation.

Divine:

The concept of the divine pertains to attributes associated with God, such as holiness, righteousness, and perfection.

Silence:

Silence refers to the absence of sound, a state of quietness that can convey peace or a deliberate withholding of speaking or acting.

God's silence:

God's silence refers to His deliberate abstention from speaking or intervening in human affairs.

Theological Insights:

Reflecting God's Silence:

Contemplating God's silence leads to understanding His sovereign plan and expectations.

A Call to Understanding: God's silence challenges our human comprehension, reminding us of His supreme wisdom and sovereignty over our affairs.

A Purposeful Pause:

Embracing the idea of God's silence underscores His sovereignty and control over His creation.

Psalms and Prophets:

Heartfelt prayers and writings found in the Psalms and prophetic scrolls, such as those of Isaiah, demonstrate how silence prompts reflection, reveals emotions, and deepens understanding.

Building Dependence:

God's silence calls us to deepen our trust and dependence on His wisdom and sovereignty during these times.

Character Refinement:

It serves as a solemn call to refine and develop our character into a better version of ourselves conforming to Christ's image.

Pursuing God's Presence:

God's silence beckons us to diligently seek an audience with Him, urging us to earnestly pursue communion and intimacy with the Almighty.

Embracing Divine Intimacy:

Divine intimacy invites us into a profound closeness with the Creator, rooted in boundless love and obedience reflective of God's nature. It encompasses various dimensions, extending beyond human understanding to include spiritual communion, visionary revelation, and experiential encounters with God.

Theological Perspectives.

God's silence unveils and unbundles significantly His dealings with mankind. It provides insight into His character and helps us understand why there are moments when He purposely withholds Himself from speaking directly or intervening in our affairs.

During this season, we are confronted with mysteries that conceal God's character, prompting us to reexamine our current perception of Him, reminding us that God's ways are far beyond our human understanding. Emphasising divine silence does not diminish His authority; But rather underscores His sovereignty.

This understanding aligns with the fact that God speaks with purpose, and His silence sets the stage for the unfolding of His sovereign agenda.

Drawing from the prayers of King David and others in scripture, we observe deliberate seasons of waiting that calls us to the place of serious pondering and a search for deeper meaning.

"The prophet Isaiah, witnessing the devastation of God's judgement on his people, desperately cried out in Isaiah 64:12, 'Will you restrain yourself at these things, O Lord? Will you keep silent and afflict us beyond measure?' His desperation captures the intricate interplay between God's silence and the painful reality of human suffering."

In Habakkuk 1:2, we hear and see the frustration of God's apparent silence in the life of Habakkuk, herein he cries: "O Lord, how long shall I cry, And You will not hear? Even cry out to You, 'Violence!' And You will not save. Significantly, deeper meanings and diverse workings that may be unclear during the season are unveiled. Instances like the 400-year gap between the Old and New Testaments sheds light on a divine pause, setting the stage for the coming of the Messiah and the establishment of His kingdom.

Excavating the Multifaceted Dimension of God's Silence.

A Call to God's Sovereign Wisdom:

God's moments of silence stir within us a desire to understand His plan. Walking in divine wisdom becomes essential to navigate these times, compelling believers to grapple with its mystery.

A Call to The Veiled Intricacies:

The concept refers to the hidden and complex aspects of God's dealings. It challenges destinies to move beyond surface-level understanding, urging for deeper depths into His ways.

A Call to Transformation:

Beyond the realm of no revelation or intervention, the silent window presents a transformative womb for encountering God beyond words. It guides on the journey of faith, speeding up a deep change from within.

A Call to Strategic Divine Workings:

This concept reveals that, during the period, strategic workings occur, challenging the assumption of inactivity. God orchestrates deeper activities during these quiet moments, offering insight into His sovereign plan.

A Call to Maturity.

It's a call to mature and toughen one's faith to endure any season in God whilst we eagerly await His unfolding events.

A call to unfold meaning and purpose:

The season unveils, in one's spiritual experience, the manifestation of layers of meaning and purposes in the divine scheme of things.

A call to Intimacy:

A deeper intimacy with God is kindled during such moments, where His awesome presence is experienced in a more tangible way. This deepens connectivity, enhances understanding, and builds a strong foundation of trust and love to underpin the relationship.

A Call to Cultivate Virtues and Values:

God's silence can be an urgent call to develop virtues such as faith, patience, longsuffering, forbearance, and more.

Here's a bit more about each of these virtues and how they can be cultivated during times of God's silence:

Faith.

Refers to the demonstration of confidence in God, His promises, ability and integrity. This involves a deep conviction of the truth of God's Word and absolute reliance on His faithfulness. Hebrew 11:1.

During God's silence maintaining trust and confidence in God, even during periods of perceived silence, is crucial for believers. It can be a testing moment, challenging one's faith and patience. However, it's during these times that the depth of our trust in God is truly revealed. By remaining steadfast and continuing to seek His presence, believers demonstrate their unwavering commitment to Him, trusting that He hears their prayers and works all things for their good, even in the silence.

PATIENCE.

Refers to our ability to endure difficult circumstances without breaking down. It involves waiting calmly for the fulfilment of God's promises. When faced with God's silence, we learn to wait patiently for His timing. We develop patience by surrendering our desires to His will, trusting that He knows the best timing for everything.

LONG-SUFFERING (ENDURANCE)

Refers to our quality of patience, endurance, or long-suffering in dealing with difficult circumstances or people. It denotes a patient and enduring attitude, especially in the face of provocation, opposition and Divine silence.

FORBEARANCE (TOLERANCE)

Refers to our ability to show patience and tolerance towards others, especially in difficult situations.

God's silence can teach us to be forbearing towards others as we seek to understand His ways. We learn to extend grace and forgiveness, knowing that we ourselves have been forgiven much.

HUMILITY.

Refers to the recognition of our dependence on God and the willingness to submit to His will. Having a modest opinion of oneself.

In times of God's silence, we are reminded of our need for Him. We humble ourselves before Him, acknowledging that His ways are higher than ours, and seek His guidance and direction.

Trust.

Refers to our firm belief in the reliability, dependability, truth, ability, confidence in God, His promises, and His character.
When faced with God's silence, we deepen our trust in Him. We learn to trust His character, His goodness, and His perfect timing, even when we cannot see the way ahead.

Hope.

Refers to our confident expectation or anticipation of something good. It signifies a hopeful outlook, trust, or assurance in God's promises and the future fulfilment of His plans. This emphasises the positive and confident expectation that believers have in God's faithfulness and the ultimate fulfilment of His purposes.

A Call unto Divine Encounter:

One is scheduled to encounter the God of heaven in a profound way within the silentude, experiencing His presence and guidance beyond the confines of words.

A Call to Wait:

This can serve as a call to wait on God and His timing, embracing the uncertainties of life without passivity. It involves actively engaging with the unknown while anticipating God's next steps. By being attentive to signs and inner guidance, it's about maintaining hope and readiness for what comes next, trusting that God is at work even in moments of silence.

A Call to Purpose.

This is a call to unveil God's hidden purposes and intentions.
One is to lay down their own will and personal agendas to God's, trusting that even in the silentude, He is working out His plans for their lives. This is to find meaning and direction in the midst of uncertainty by aligning one's purpose with God's divine will.

A Call to Surrender.

This may signal the call to release fears, doubts, and anxieties into God's hands.

It's to trust fully in God's goodness, wisdom, and sovereignty, even when circumstances are unclear or challenging. Surrendering to God means letting go of the need for control and finding peace in the assurance that God is in control.

A Call to Renewal:

This may serve as a call to spiritual renewal and transformation.
This allows God's transformative work to bring about the shifts required for the new phase of assignment. It's about letting go of old ways, habits, and attitudes to make space for God to renew and deepen one's sense of purpose and spiritual vitality.

A Language of God:

God's silentude is a language of its own—one that reveals the layers of God's multifaceted intents and purposes beyond human comprehension. It speaks with clarity and insight, shedding light on the intricate workings of His plan for humanity and creation, inviting us to participate in His unfolding plan for the world.

A Comfort in Silence:

Despite the absence of audible words, one can find comfort in the silent assurance of God's presence.

It's a reminder that God is always at work, even in the quietest moments. In times of uncertainty or waiting, one can trust in God's faithfulness and His perfect will being carried out in their lives.

The Journey of Faith:

Ultimately, God's silence is a call to walk on the water with Him. A journey of faith which challenges us to trust in His goodness, rest in His sovereignty, and walk in obedience even when the storm is life threatening.

As we navigate the seasons of God's silence, may we find strength in His promises, wisdom in His ways, and a renewed sense of hope that anchors our souls in His unchanging love in Jesus mighty name.

The Biblical Perspective Of God's Silence.

Abraham's Test of Faith.

In Genesis 22, Abraham's unwavering trust is tested as he prepares to sacrifice his son Isaac. Despite God's silence, Abraham obediently follows through, demonstrating profound faith in God's redemptive plan.

Job's Resilience in Suffering.

Job's enduring faith during intense suffering showcases his unwavering commitment to God, even amidst divine silence. Despite the absence of clear answers, Job remains steadfast, highlighting resilience in times of adversity.

The Psalmist's Cry for Presence.

Psalm 42 portrays the Psalmist's longing for God's presence amidst divine silence. Despite the lack of immediate response, the Psalmist's soul thirsts for God, revealing an enduring pursuit of intimacy.

Hosea's Divine Pursuit:

Prophet Hosea's narrative reflects God's relentless pursuit of His people, even in seasons of silence. Hosea 2:14 illustrates God's promise to speak comfortingly to His people, demonstrating His enduring love and commitment. Jesus' Submission to God's Plan In Matthew 26, Jesus exemplifies submission to the Father's will despite facing betrayal and abandonment. Amidst apparent silence, Jesus remains steadfast, showcasing unwavering obedience to God's plan.

In conclusion, the weight of God's silence cannot be underestimated, as it beckons us to seek insight and meaning amidst the quietude, nurturing enduring faith and trust in His sovereign plan. These biblical examples stand as beacons of light, guiding believers through the mysterious yet profound seasons of God's silence. Through their narratives, we are reminded that in the hush, God is at work, orchestrating His purposes, refining our faith, and drawing us closer to Himself. May we, like Abraham, Job, the Psalmist, Hosea, and Jesus, discover strength and perseverance in the midst of God's purposeful silence, assured that His plans are always for our ultimate good, revealing His glory.

Highlights.

Mystery and Divine Silence:

The concept of mystery refers to something difficult to understand or explain. Divine silence refers to God's purposeful withholding of Himself from speaking or intervening.

Pondering and Understanding:

Reflecting on God's silence can lead to understanding His intentions and expectations.

It challenges human comprehension, emphasising God's wisdom and sovereignty.

Purpose and Sovereignty:

Divine silence emphasises God's sovereignty and control.
It is not His absence but a deliberate withholding for specific reasons.

Scriptural Examples:

Examples from the Psalms and Isaiah show how silence encourages reflection and reveals emotions.

Building Dependence:

Believers are called to deepen their trust and dependence on God during silent times.

Character Refinement.

God's silence is a call to grow and develop into a better version of oneself.

Seeking God:

It urges believers to earnestly seek an audience with God.

Reflection and Intimacy:

Divine silence prompts reflection on faith and deepens intimacy with God.

Theological Perspectives.

Divine silence reveals significant aspects of God's character and dealings with humanity. It challenges believers to reexamine their perception of God.

God's Purposeful Speaking:

God speaks with purpose, setting the stage for His agenda.

Season of Waiting:

Scriptures show deliberate seasons of waiting, urging believers to ponder deeply.

Desperation and Interplay:

Examples from Isaiah and Habakkuk show the interplay between God's silence and human suffering.

Multiple Purposes:

The season of divine pause serves various purposes within God's plan.

Cultivating Virtues:

God's silence teaches virtues such as faith, patience, longsuffering, forbearance, humility, trust, and hope.

Encounter and Renewal:

Believers encounter God so deeply in silence, leading to renewal and deeper faith.

Chapter 3

God Breaks the Silence

There comes a time in life when the heavens seem to hold their breath, and the earth awaits in anticipation. It is a time when the voice of prayers seems to linger unanswered, and the heavens appear veiled in silence. Yet, in the midst of this apparent quietude, there lies a divine orchestration, a purposeful pause in the experiences of life.

For it is in these moments of silence that God speaks the loudest. It is when His voice breaks through the stillness, piercing the darkness with the light of His voice. His presence is felt, His guidance is sought.

In "God Breaks the Silence," we embark on a profound journey of discovery, delving deep into the mysteries of God's voice. We uncover the secrets veiled within His silence and the extraordinary revelations that unfold when He chooses to speak. Let us approach with open hearts and attentive ears, for within the silence, His voice stands ready to break through, illuminating our path with God's wisdom and grace.

When God eventually breaks the silence, it's a language of its own. It's a sign and mark of divine accomplishment, divine vindication, a signal to an answered prayer. A mark and sign of readiness.

It's a sign of divine preservation and covering from the evil one and danger, a mark of perceived faith activated, a mark of maturity and growth attained, a mark of prophetic timing reached, a sign and mark of divine purpose and plan received.

It's a sign of brokenness, yieldedness, and surrender perceived, a mark that alignment to the kingdom agenda is in place, a sign and mark of repentance from a rebellious state, a mark and sign of growth and maturity attained.

It's a sign of divine revelation accessed and patterns obtained."

In Psalm 78:65-72, we see the Almighty God being portrayed as a mighty warrior who suddenly awakes from His sleep, ready to confront His enemies head-on.

The Lord's sudden act isn't merely a stirring, but a deliberate resurgence, similar to a warrior under the influence of strong wine, prepared to unleash perpetual disgrace upon His enemies. The Scriptures underscore divine timing, illustrating the relevance of the gap between God's silence and His resurgence. It establishes the fact that this isn't a neglect, but an orchestration of a Sovereign Plan.

Therefore, it is paramount you take into full account your own season of God's quietness, appreciate its relevance, and accept it as God's plan, even as revealed in Psalm 78. It's therefore important to note that these are not random interruptions but a deliberate pause, serving as waypoints and markers in the unfolding program of God.

Going through moments of God's silence is a deep spiritual experience; thoughts of despair, discouragement, and feelings of abandonment may set in, finding rhythm with the sentiments expressed by the Israelites in Psalm 137:1-4.

By the rivers of Babylon,
There we sat down, yea, we wept
When we remembered Zion.
We hang our harps
Upon the willows in the midst of it.
For there, those who carried us away captive asked of us a song,
And those who plundered us requested mirth,
Saying, "Sing us one of the songs of Zion!"
How shall we sing the Lord's song
In a foreign land?

The accounts vividly portray the Israelites in a state of God's silence, despairing and feeling abandoned and disconnected in Babylonian captivity. They remembered Zion, the place of the covenant, the burial place of their patriarchs and prophets of old, their homeland, sitting by the rivers of Babylon they wept, hung their harps upon the willows, unable to find the joy and melody of their songs in a foreign land. In their hearts, they questioned, 'How shall we sing the Lord's song in a foreign land?' reflecting the deep anguish and longing for the presence of God, feeling disconnected and lost in a land far from their spiritual home.

God Breaks The Silence.

When God's purpose for the window of his silence is accomplished as determined, He speaks again, His mighty deeds manifest. Prayers find answers, victories from unseen battles unfold, joy renewed, and new songs of praise arise. It is a time of restored order, unlike anything before. The clouds part to herald a new dawn in the lives of humanity.

Scriptures illustrate moments when God broke the silence, showcasing His character and sovereign authority.

After over 400 years of servitude and silence in Egyptian bondage, God hears the cries of the Israelites and speaks to Moses at the back side of the desert , specifically on Mt Horeb from a burning bush, setting the stage for their exodus.

Similarly, in her state of barrenness and deep distress, Hannah prayed fervently for a child. After a long period of apparent silence, God remembered her and blessed her with Samuel, who became a great prophet in Israel.

Further Biblical Examples.

The Exile and its Return.

During the exile in Babylon, the Israelites felt abandoned and in silence. Yet, God spoke through prophets like Isaiah and Jeremiah, promising restoration and their return to their homeland.

Esther's Intercession.

In the face of imminent danger, Esther fasted and prayed with her people. God intervened , orchestrating events behind the scenes to deliver the Jews from destruction.

The Period of the Judges.

After Joshua's death, a period of silence emerged as the Israelites faced cycles of rebellion and captivity. God spoke again by raising up judges and deliverers like Deborah, Gideon, and Samson to lead them to victory and to comply with His agenda.

The Prophetic Silence Before Isaiah's Ministry.

There was a prophetic season of silence in Isaiah's life before his ministry fully emerged. During this period, there was no record of any divine revelation. However, God spoke to the prophet dramatically in Isaiah chapter 6 through a vision encounter. This marked the end of the silent period and the commencement of Isaiah's prophetic assignment.

The Intertestamental Silent Gap:

Between the Old and New Testaments, there was a period of silence in terms of prophetic voices.

However, God broke this silence with the coming of John the Baptist, who served as the forerunner preparing the way for the arrival of the Messiah, as described in Matthew 3. This marked a pivotal moment in history, signalling the fulfilment of ancient prophecies and the beginning of a new era with the arrival of Jesus Christ.

THE SILENCE BEFORE JESUS' PUBLIC MINISTRY.

There exists a silent gap in the Gospels regarding Jesus' life between His childhood and public ministry. God breaks the silence with John's baptism, marking the commencement of His public ministry. During His crucifixion, Jesus endured a profound sense of neglect and abandonment by the Father. Yet, His resurrection signifies God's voice echoing once more.

A CALL TO REPENTANCE.

God's silence and apparent inactivity can signal the need for repentance. It's a call to self-examination. Sin of any form blocks God's voice and restrains His intervention.

Isaiah 59:2 renders, "But your iniquities have separated you from your God; And your sins have hidden His face from you, So that He can not hear.

Proverbs 28:9 states, "If one turns away his ear from hearing the law, even his prayer is an abomination." Ignoring God's teachings and living in disobedience can render prayers unacceptable. These biblical references illustrate how sin can create a barrier to hearing God's voice and experiencing His active intervention.

The first step to repentance involves a deliberate change of mind and attitude. It is in this contrite state of heart that opens one up to the frequency of God's voice, inviting seasons of refreshing from His presence.

A Call to Kingdom Alignment:

When the demands and promptings of God's silence are carried out, a necessary alignment takes place. A life once veering off its destined course finds its bearings. Aligning with God's prophetic purposes and agenda is a platform to the voice of the Lord and His interventions.

Let's explore the period leading to Samuel's emergence, preceded by a season of no record of revelation from God. Samuel's call initiated a new phase of prophetic revelation 1 Samuel 3. His emergence is connected with Hannah's alignment, as found in 1 Samuel 1:1-20, focusing on Hannah's prayer and vow in verses 9-18, and the birth of Samuel subsequently in 1 Samuel 1:19-28. Explains how Hannah's silent cry, desperation, and eventual alignment with God's purpose led to the birth of Samuel the prophet and priest.

The Appointed Time.

Exploring divine schedules helps us understand and discern God's timing and plans for events as they relate to humanity, touching every sphere of human existence.

Here are a few windows to peer through:

God's Sovereignty.:

Recognizing God's sovereignty over all things means understanding that His timing is perfect and His plans are ultimately fulfilled according to His will.

Prophetic Timing.:

Throughout history, God has used prophets to announce His plans and timing for various events. Studying prophecy offers insights into God's schedule.

Biblical Examples:

The Bible contains numerous examples of God's timing and schedules, illustrating His sovereignty over events and His faithfulness in fulfilling prophecies. Examples include the precise timing of Jesus' birth in fulfilment of Old Testament prophecies, the timing of key events in the lives of biblical figures such as Abraham, Moses, and David, and the fulfilment of prophetic promises throughout biblical history. These examples highlight God's control over time and His fulfilment of His purposes according to His divine schedule.

Personal Journey:

Understanding God's timing in our personal lives is indeed a journey filled with challenges, but it's also incredibly rewarding. As we reflect on past experiences and discern God's leading, we gain clarity on His schedule for our lives.

Sometimes, it may seem like things are not happening according to our timeline, but looking back, we often see how God's timing was perfect, even if it didn't align with our expectations. Trusting in His timing requires patience, faith, and a willingness to surrender our own plans to His greater purpose. Through this process, we grow closer to God, deepen our faith, and experience the fulfilment of His promises in our lives.

In Genesis 18:9-10, Abraham encountered divine visitors. "Where is Sarah, your wife?" they asked. Abraham replied, "Here, in the tent." Then came the prophetic verdict, "I will certainly return to you according to the time of life, and behold, Sarah your wife shall have a son." Referencing Genesis 21, Sarah gives birth to the promised son, Isaac, after 25 years of God's Silence. Galatians 4:4 further illuminates, "But when the fullness of time had come, God sent forth His Son, born of a woman, born under the law." This explains God's timing as it relates to His prophetic calendar.

A Call to the Test of Love:

During seasons of God's silence, one is reminded of the dialogue between Jesus and Peter in John 21:15-17. After Peter's denial of Jesus, this conversation unfolds as a profound moment of restoration and reaffirmation of love. Jesus asks Peter three times, "Do you love Me?" Each time, Peter responded affirmatively, expressing his love for the Lord. This exchange symbolises the deepening of Peter's commitment and highlights the transformative power of love amidst silence.

Exploring further, this passage reveals that love is not merely a feeling but a commitment, a choice and preference demonstrated through action. In moments of God's silence, our love for God is tested and proven through our obedience, trust, and perseverance. It's in these silent seasons that our faith is refined, and our relationship with God is strengthened as we continue to love and serve Him faithfully

A Call to Growth And Maturity:

God's silence is a call to growth and maturity, signalling a time for individuals to acquire the necessary skills and wisdom to effectively carry out the next phase of God's plan. A prime example of this is evident in the prophetic arrangement surrounding John the Baptist and Jesus' earthly ministry.

Despite Zechariah and Elizabeth's advanced age, God waited for the right time before Mary conceived the Messiah. John the Baptist, too, remained in the silent desert until the appointed time of his public appearance. As Luke 1:80 states, "And the child grew and became strong in spirit, and he was in the wilderness until the day of his public appearance to Israel."

In God's divine plan, growth is indeed a prerequisite for fulfilling His agenda. This period of growth and preparation allowed John to develop spiritually and emotionally, equipping him for the significant role he would play in preparing the way for Jesus' ministry. Likewise, in our own lives, God's silence may serve as an opportunity for us to grow and mature, preparing us for the tasks and responsibilities He has in store for us.

A Season of Revelation:

Revelations are received in God's presence, where deep insights and understanding beyond the ordinary are accessed. It is during these moments that God imparts secrets of Himself and His ways. God who is the source of revelation, encounters Adam in the tranquil of the day to reveal aspects of His will. During the season of God's silence on Mount Sinai, Moses encountered significant revelations, as detailed in the book of Exodus 19-20. Likewise, Apostle Paul experienced profound revelations during his time in the deserts of Arabia after his conversion, as referenced in Galatians 1:17.

Also, behind the prison bars of silence, he penned down the epistles according to Ephesians, Philippians, Colossians, and Philemon, which contain insights into the mysteries of the kingdom of God. He explains that these mysteries were made known to him by revelation.

A Call To Transformation.

God accomplishes a transformative process in one's life during the season of His silence, wherein the mind emerges fundamentally renewed.

Jacob encounters an Angel in solitude, as referenced in Genesis 32:22-32, he wrestled with the Angel until the breaking of day, culminating in the change of his name from Jacob to Israel. This change signified his transformation, as highlighted in Hosea 12:4, "He struggled with the angel and prevailed; he wept and sought his favour. He met God at Bethel, and there God spoke with us."

This event does not just symbolise Jacob's personal and spiritual growth but also serves as a testament to the transformative power that comes through wrestling with the divine in moments of solitude.

Fighting Unseen Battles and Averting Certain Dangers.

God fights battles that relate to His will for your life and averts demonic dangers programmed. He clears the way for you during this period.

Matthew 2:13-15:

"When they had gone, an angel of the Lord appeared to Joseph in a dream. 'Get up,' he said, 'take the child and his mother and escape to Egypt. Stay there until I tell you, for Herod is going to search for the child to kill him.

' So he got up, took the child and his mother during the night and left for Egypt, where he stayed until the death of Herod. And so was fulfilled what the Lord had said through the prophet: 'Out of Egypt I called my son.'"

Matthew 2:19-20:
"After Herod died, an angel of the Lord appeared in a dream to Joseph in Egypt and said, 'Get up, take the child and his mother and go to the land of Israel, for those who were trying to take the child's life are dead.'"

We see God's silent intervention in the lives of Joseph, Mary, and Jesus to protect baby Jesus from danger.

The threat from Herod represents an unseen battle, a demonic plot to destroy Jesus, the Messiah. This reflects the broader spiritual warfare believers often face. God's intervention through the angel shows that He is aware of these hidden dangers and provides the means to avert them.

The flight to Egypt and the subsequent return to Israel fulfil prophecies, underscoring that God's plans are sovereign and cannot be thwarted by human or demonic schemes. This gives believers confidence that God fights in moments of His silence behind the scenes .

Giving the Devil No Place" involves key actions for believers

ACTIVELY RESIST SIN.

This includes resisting sinful behaviours, thoughts, and influences that go against God's will.

Guard Your Heart and Mind.

Be vigilant in protecting your heart and mind from anything that contradicts God's truth and righteousness.

Cultivate a Lifestyle of Prayer.

Regular, consistent heartfelt prayer strengthens your relationship with God and helps you stay aligned with His will.

Staying in God's Word.

Remaining rooted in God's Word is not a suggestion but a daily necessity for personal transformation and the maintenance of victory in the conflicts of life.

The Importance of the Word.

The Word of God is the foundation for one's life. It is a timeless truth and principle for navigating life's challenges and putting the devil in his rightful place.

The Word as a Guide.

Staying rooted in God's Word means turning to the Scriptures for direction in every aspect of life. It offers clear instructions on how to live a life that pleases God and aligns with His purposes.

Renewing the Mind.

Remaining rooted in God's Word involves renewing the mind with its principles. Romans 12:2 urges believers, "Do not be conformed to this world, but be ye transformed by the renewal of your mind, that you may discern what the will of God is, what is that good and acceptable and perfect.

Foundation for Faith.

A strong foundation in the Word ignites faith and trust in God, even in challenging times. Psalm 18:30 affirms, "This God, His way is perfect; the word of the Lord proves true; he is a shield for all those who take refuge in him.

Discerning God's Will.

By remaining rooted in Scripture, we can develop discernment to recognize God's will in various situations. Proverbs 3:5-6 encourages, "Trust in the Lord with all your heart, and do not lean on your own understanding. In all your ways acknowledge him, and he will direct your path.

In essence, "Giving the Devil No Place" is a call to stand firm in your faith, actively resisting the forces of darkness, and living in a way that brings honour to God. It reminds us that through Christ, we have the power to overcome evil and walk in righteousness. This is a powerful encouragement for all who follow Christ and seek to live a life that reflects His grace and glory.

Highlights.

God's Active Intervention:
God is portrayed as a mighty warrior in Psalm 78:65-72, ready to confront enemies.

His act of resurgence is deliberate and purposeful.

Timing and Purpose:

God's timing between silence and intervention illustrates His plan. Silence is not neglect but part of His unfolding Sovereign Plan.

Understanding God's Silence:

Important to recognize and accept seasons of God's quietness. They serve as markers in His plan, not random interruptions.

Examples of Silence in Scripture:

Israelites' despair in Babylonian captivity (Psalm 137:1-4). Hannah's prayer and the birth of Samuel after a period of silence.

Biblical Examples:

Restoration promises in Babylon.

Esther's intercession and God's intervention.
Period of judges and prophetic silence before Isaiah.
The gap between the Old and New Testaments.
Silence before Jesus' ministry.

Spiritual Responses to Silence.

Call to repentance for sin as a barrier.
Aligning with God's purposes to understand His voice.
Recognizing God's appointed times for fulfilment.

Tests and Growth in Silence.

Silence tests and deepens one's love and faith.
Refining process for growth and maturity during silent seasons.

Demonic Opposition and Resistance.

Satan's tactics to hinder God's work and cause silence is dealt with.
Daniel's prayer and the battle with demonic forces.

Biblical Examples Continued.

The period of exile in Babylon, showing Israel's hope in the midst of silence. Esther's intercession and God's hidden work to save His people. The judges' era, marked by silence before God raised deliverers. Isaiah's prophetic silence before his ministry, ended by a dramatic vision.

The intertestamental period, followed by John the Baptist's arrival.

Jesus' Ministry and Silence.

Jesus' preparation period before His public ministry.
His silence during the crucifixion, followed by the resurrection as God's voice.

Call to Repentance and Alignment.

Sin as a barrier to hearing God's voice and experiencing
His intervention. Aligning with God's purposes to understand His voice and plan.

Appointed Times and Promises.

Waiting for God's appointed time for the fulfilment of his promises. The story of Abraham and Sarah, waiting for the birth of Isaac. The fullness of time when God sent Jesus, fulfilling His plan of salvation.

Tests of Love and Growth.

Silence as a test of love, deepening one's faith and relationship with God. Growth and maturity through the refining process of silent seasons.

Revelation in Silence.

Deep insights and understanding received in the solitude of God's presence. Examples include Moses on Mount Sinai and Apostle Paul's revelations.

Overcoming Demonic Opposition.

Satan's tactics to hinder God's work through demonic strongholds. Daniel's prayer and the battle with the prince of Persia, showing victory over darkness.

Chapter 4

The Purpose of God's Silence

During the season of God's silence or disconnect, a purposeful work is accomplished behind the scenes in the lives of individuals, families, cities, churches, and nations, according to God's predetermined counsel. God may be quiet in one area of someone's life while speaking in different aspects of that life.

This may signal a call to preparation, refinement, and alignment with God's kingdom placement for individuals, families, churches, nations, and others, ultimately revealing His will.

The Multifaceted Agenda of God's Silence

Revelation 8:1-6… Illustrates and Highlights the Experience

When He opened the seventh seal, there was silence in heaven for about half an hour. And I saw the seven angels who stand before God, and to them were given seven trumpets. Then another angel, having a golden censer, came and stood at the altar. He was given so much incense that he should offer it with the prayers of all the saints upon the golden altar which was before the throne. And the smoke of the incense, with the prayers of the saints, ascended before God from the angel's hand. Then the angel took the censer, filled it with fire from the altar, and threw it to the earth. And there were noises, thunderings, lightnings, and an earthquake. So the seven angels who had the seven trumpets prepared themselves to sound.

Let's take a prophetic walk through the sequence of events that took place in John's vision according to the scripture under consideration:

The Lamb opened the seventh seal and ushered in a moment of silence in heaven for about half an hour. During this period, seven angels came to stand before God, who were given seven trumpets.

Another angel, holding a golden censer, comes and stands at the altar. This angel was given much incense to offer with the prayers of all the saints upon the golden altar before the throne. The smoke of the incense, mingled with the prayers of the saints, ascended before God.

The angel takes the censer, fills it with fire from the altar, and throws it to the earth, resulting in noises, thunderings, lightnings, and an earthquake. The seven angels who were given the seven trumpets prepare themselves to sound. All these taking place within the silent window in heaven.

This sequence of events reveals how the voice of God's silentude sets the stage for the manifestation of His next Agenda.

The Discovery of Purpose.

In the quietness of God's presence, divine purposes unfold. Through prayer, holy solemnity, and in seeking of His will, one can understand the path laid out by God.

God's Sovereign Design.

God's plan for each person's life is not randomly picked but intentionally crafted. It involves intricate details, processes, and specific steps to find fulfilment.

Preparation and Refinement.

Silence often serves as a time of preparation and refinement.
God moulds and shapes individuals, refining their character and faith for the tasks ahead.

Alignment with God's Plan.

Individuals, families, businesses, churches and nations must align themselves with God's will, become vessels for His purposes.

This alignment leads to a deeper understanding of His plan and a willingness to walk in obedience for its execution.

Fulfilment in Lives.

Ultimately, God's plan leads to the fulfilment of His purposes in one's life. Whether it's through ministry, relationships, or other areas, His plan unfolds in remarkable ways.

Impact on Families.

Families experience moments of God's quietude working out His plan. Through understanding of purpose, wisdom, unity, love, and faithfulness to God and each other, families become beacons of His light.

Blessings for Churches.

Churches that follow God's plan experience growth, unity, and spiritual depth. God empowers them to fulfil their assignment, impact communities for His glory.

Transformation of Nations.

When nations turn to God and align with His purposes, transformation occurs and destiny finds its path to accomplishment . History is filled with examples of nations experiencing revivals, renewals, and civilizations after seeking God's plan.

Divine Appointments and Opportunities.

During the seasons of silence, God orchestrates appointments and opportunities.

These moments lead to opened doors , provision, and strategic connections for His purposes to unfold.

Walking in Faith and Obedience.

Central to discovering God's plan is walking in faith and obedience to fulfil it.

It requires trust in His timing, surrender to His will, and boldness to step into the unknown.

Testimony of God's Faithfulness.

As individuals, families, churches, and nations walk in God's plan, they become testaments of His faithfulness.

Others witness the work of God and are drawn to Him through these testimonies.

The Testing and Refining of Faith.

Abraham.

Abraham's Test of Faith in Genesis 22:1-19.
God tested Abraham's faith by asking him to sacrifice his son, Isaac. Abraham's willingness to sacrifice Isaac demonstrates His deep trust in God's plan, even in the face of divine silence.

God uses this test as a testament, Abraham's faith was refined and strengthened, solidifying his trust and reliance on God.

Joseph.

Preparation and Perseverance in Genesis 37-50
Joseph's time of obscurity and suffering in slavery and prison in the face of divine silentude, served as preparation for his role as a leader in Egypt.

He endured years of hardship with patience and perseverance, ultimately fulfilling God's plan to save his family and many others.

Moses.

Leading the Israelites in Exodus.
Moses faced numerous challenges, including the stubbornness of the Israelites and the daunting task of leading them out of Egypt.

Despite the trials, Moses remained steadfast in following God's guidance, trusting in His provision and leading.

DAVID.

FROM THE SHEEPFOLD TO KINGSHIP
1 SAMUEL, PSALMS.
From a humble shepherd boy to the place of a monarch, David confronted trials, including persecution from Saul and the consequences of his own sins. His psalms resonate with a deep trust in God during testing times. (1 Samuel, Psalms)

DANIEL.

FAITH IN THE FACE OF PERSECUTION IN DANIEL 6.
Daniel refusing to compromise his faith led to his facing the lion's den. His unwavering trust in God's protection resulted in a miraculous deliverance from the lion's Den. Daniel 6..

PETER.

DENIAL AND REDEMPTION IN MATTHEW 26:69-75.
Peter's denial of Jesus during His trial was a severe test of his faith. Despite this failure, Peter was restored by Jesus and later emerged as a key figure in spreading the gospel.

PAUL.

A PERSECUTOR TO APOSTOLIC ACTS AND EPISTLES.
Paul's transformation from a persecutor of Christians to a fervent apostle demonstrates the power of God's grace. Despite his imprisonment, persecution, and trials, Paul's faith endured, and he continued to spread the gospel.

These biblical characters illustrate the testing and refinement of faith, demonstrating how trust in God can endure challenging moments.

Preparation for a Greater Calling.

Biblical players such as Joseph and David experienced seasons of apparent silence or obscurity before assuming significant roles. Those moments served as a preparatory phase for all those destined for greater calling or purpose in God's scheme of things.
Genesis 37-41; 1 Samuel 16.

Strategic Positioning.

God strategically positions individuals to accomplish purpose. The accounts of Esther in chapter 2 highlights God's strategic positioning for specific assignments.

Esther's rise to become a queen was part of God's plan to save the Jewish people from destruction.

Averting Unseen Danger.

Sometimes God remains silent to protect us from unforeseen dangers or premature outcomes. His perfect timing ensures that His plans unfold in the best possible way, even if it means temporarily withholding His voice or intervention.

Joseph's safeguarding from potential harm orchestrated by his brothers ***Genesis 37-50.***

Divine Dependency.

God's silence, a call to the school of divine dependency, where one learns total reliance on Him.

By withholding His voice or intervention, He teaches us to seek Him diligently, recognizing that God alone holds the solutions to life's challenges.

Psalm 62 exemplifies total trust in God, finding solace in His silence while eagerly awaiting His salvation.

Waiting On God's Revelation.

Scripture clarifies God's time for action. His season of silence isn't empty; it's a time of waiting expectantly for the manifestation and revelation of His plans. **Habakkuk 2:3** beautifully encapsulates this way,

For the vision is yet for an appointed time.
But at the end, it will speak, and it will not lie.
Though it tarries, wait for it.
Because it will surely come,
It will not tarry.

Cultivating Patience and Perseverance.

In times of God's silence, one is encouraged to cultivate virtues of patience and perseverance, as highlighted throughout scripture. The narrative of Abraham waiting for the promised son exemplifies this, illustrating how the waiting period becomes fertile ground for the growth of these qualities. This narrative is a powerful reminder of the importance of patience and perseverance in the journey of faith, as mentioned in **Hebrews 6:15.**

Divine Alignment and Attunement.

During God's silence He works behind the scenes to align individuals, families, businesses, institutions, churches, and nations with His kingdom plan to find expression within a cosmic context.

Revealing His Sovereignty.

God's silence becomes an opportunity for one to grow in humility, trust, and active participation in His plan. Instead of discouragement, it fosters trust in God's perfect timing and wisdom.

We can rest assured that God works for our good, revealing His glory even in the midst of chaotic circumstances. This emphasises how God's sovereignty transforms us, leading to growth and trust in His unseen but purposeful work. It encourages active participation in His plan and guiding hand.

In conclusion, these examples reveal how God's apparent silence is not empty but purposeful. It serves to mould character, prepare for greater callings, cultivate patience and perseverance, strategically position individuals, protect them from unseen dangers, teach dependency, await God's revelation, align with divine purposes, and reveal His sovereignty over all things.

Highlights.

Realisation of Purpose.

In God's silence, divine purposes can be realised through prayer and seeking His will.

God's Sovereign Design.

God's plan for each person's life is intentional, with specific steps for fulfilment.

Preparation and Refinement.

Silence serves as a time of preparation and refinement of character and faith.

Alignment with God's Plan.

Aligning with God's will lead to a deeper understanding of His plan and obedience.

Fulfilment in Lives.

God's plan ultimately leads to the fulfilment of His purposes in people's lives.

The Impact on Families.

Families experience moments of God's silence as opportunities for growth and unity.

Transformation of Nations.

Nations turning to God and His purposes experience revival and blessings.

Divine Appointments and Opportunities.

God orchestrates appointments and opportunities for His purposes.

Walking in Faith and Obedience.

Discovering God's plan requires trust, surrender, and boldness to step into the unknown.

Testimony of God's Faithfulness.

Those following God's plan become testimonies of His faithfulness to draw others to Him.

Testing and Refining of Faith.

Biblical examples like Abraham, Joseph, Moses, David, Daniel, Peter, and Paul show how faith is tested and refined.

Preparation for a Greater Calling.

Seasons of silence often precede significant roles or callings in God's plan.

The Strategic Positioning.

God positions individuals strategically, like Esther, for specific purposes.

Averting Unseen Danger.

God's silence sometimes protects from unforeseen dangers, ensuring His plans unfold at the time appointed.

Chapter 5

Biblical Players

(Part I)

Romans 15:4 states, "For whatsoever things were written aforetime were written for our learning, that we through patience and comfort of the scriptures might have hope." In the same vein **Hebrews 6:12** exhorts us, "That ye be not slothful, but followers of them who through faith and patience inherit the promises."

These accounts illuminate the importance of learning from the experiences of those who came before us in the faith journey. By gleaning from their narratives of faith, patience, comfort even in the face of adversity, and hope in obtaining God's promises, we find encouragement as we look unto Jesus, the author and finisher of our faith.

Embarking on an expedition through the eyes of Job and others who experienced the depths of God's silence, we encounter Job, described as a righteous and blameless man living in the land of Uz, who faced unimaginable trials and suffering. In the midst of these challenges, Job finds himself in the window of God's silence. He cries out to the heavens for an explanation to understand, yet it was met with a divine no-show.

Adding to his anguish, Job's friends, in their attempts to make sense of his suffering, accused him of possible hidden sin. Despite their doubts, Job stood firm in his integrity and continued to seek an audience with the Almighty God, longing for understanding and vindication.

Amidst his desperate cries, there was no immediate response from above. Nevertheless, Job held onto his faith, as expressed in Job 13:15, "Though He slay me, yet will I trust in Him."

In *Job 23:8-9*, he expresses his desire to find God and understand His ways.

"Look, I go forward, but he is not there,
and backward, but I cannot perceive him;
on the left hand I seek him, but I cannot behold him;
I turn to the right, but I cannot see him.

Through the silence, Job continued to cling to God's wisdom and sovereignty, knowing that God's ways are far beyond human understanding.

God eventually breaks the silence, appearing to Job in a whirlwind in *Job 38-41.* He speaks of the wonders of creation and His sovereignty over all things. Through the encounter, Job gains a deeper understanding of God's majesty and the limitations of human understanding.

Job stands as a timeless symbol and archetype for generations. Though passed on, yet his story continues to speak volumes, declaring that God's silence does not equate to abandonment, but rather serves as a call to trust in His sovereignty and wisdom, even when we cannot see or understand His ways. Job's unwavering faith and patience amidst silence ultimately led to the restoration of his fortunes and a deeper revelation of God's majesty.

This perspective draws inspiration from Job's relentless pursuit for an audience with God, urging us to consider our own desire for intimacy with the Almighty. It prompts reflection on the depth of relationship we seek with God and the yearning for closeness that Job's accounts portray.

Just as Job deeply desired an encounter with God, one is encouraged to seek communion with Him, yearning for His presence, guidance, and justice in their lives. This desire for intimacy with God is not solely about seeking answers but a sincere longing to be in His presence, fully acknowledging and recognizing His sovereignty over all things.

Through the pursuit of intimacy with God, one can cultivate a deep and meaningful relationship with Him, finding strength and joy unspeakable in His ever-abiding presence.

In *Psalms 17:1*, David stands before God's sovereign presence to plead his case, and similar expressions reverberate, revealing the shared human longing for an audience with God, expressing the desire for His attention and justice.

This experience extends beyond the Old Testament, as Jesus highlights seeking God's audience in His teachings on prayer, as seen in *Matthew 7:7*.

THE OTHER WITH JOB ON THE JOURNEY.

Let's explore how the prophetic Psalms offer significant guidance through times of God's silence.

EMOTIONS IN THE PSALMS:

The Psalms serve as a profound reflection of a diverse range of human emotions, from despair to exuberant praise. They teach us the importance of being honest with God about how we feel, including moments of confusion, anger, and feeling forsaken.

In *Psalm 22*, the psalmist cries out, "My God, my God, why have you forsaken me?" These very words were later echoed by Jesus Christ on the cross. Following His example, we are encouraged to bring our raw emotions to God in prayer, knowing that our Advocate understands our weaknesses, struggles, and the depths of our hearts.

Being honest with God deepens our relationship with Him and opens the door to experience His comfort, healing, and guidance in the face of silence. It reminds us that we can pour out our hearts before Him, trusting in His unfailing love and understanding.

Finding Hope in Waiting.

Psalm 40:1-3 emphasises the importance of patiently waiting for the Lord, recognizing that He hears our cries and rescues us from despair. This underscores that waiting on God is an active expression of faith, leading to personal growth, refinement, and a deepening trust in His faithfulness. Through this waiting period, our focus shifts from our circumstances to depend on God's integrity.

Assurance of God's Presence:

The narratives of Job and the Psalms reassure us of God's continual presence, even during times of His apparent silence. Although we may not always sense Him or comprehend His ways, we can have confidence of his ever abiding presence with us.

Psalm 46:10 encourages us to "Be still, and know that He is God," urging us to place our trust in His sovereign wisdom. This reassures us that we are never abandoned, even in moments of silence, as God works out His purposes for our lives behind the scenes.

The narrative of Elijah in the desert, particularly in 1 Kings 19, illustrates the significance of God's silence. Despite the absence of overt communication, God meets Elijah unexpectedly, revealing His presence and guidance in unexpected ways.

Divine Encounter and Testing.

After Elijah's dramatic victory over the prophets of Baal on Mount Carmel, he finds himself in the desert place, exhausted both physically, emotionally and spiritually. God's silence during this season was his test case, challenging His faith and determination.

A Shift from The Spectacular to Stillness.

Before his wilderness experience, Elijah witnessed a powerful display of God's presence and power, including physical fire coming down from heaven. Now in the desert, God manifests in a "gentle whisper" *-1 Kings 19:12*, emphasising the shift from the spectacular to the still and small voice.

Encouragement in Solitude.

Elijah's experience in the desert place signifies the profound encounters that can happen in moments of God's silence. When he fled to the wilderness, exhausted and discouraged,

In the depths of his solitude, Elijah encountered God in a still, small voice *1 Kings 19:12*. This gentle whisper amidst the silence spoke volumes to Elijah's soul, providing comfort, direction, and encouragement. It was in this quiet place that Elijah found strength to continue his journey, reassured of God's presence and direction.

Elijah's narrative teaches us that in moments of solitude and apparent silence, God speaks to us in diverse ways. It is often in these quiet places that we can hear His voice most clearly. This encourages us to embrace times of divine discontent as opportunities for His encounters, where God speaks to our hearts, and provides the strength we need to press on in faith.

Learning Absolute Dependence on God.

The silence is a learning phase for absolute dependence on God. Elijah's experience teaches us that our authority and power comes directly from God, and one cannot rely on their abilities or past experiences.

When faced with God's silence, Elijah was stripped off the familiar manifestations of God's power that he was used to or had witnessed in the past—the fire, the earthquake, and the wind. Instead, he encountered God in a gentle whisper, highlighting the need for a deeper and total dependence on God's leading.

This period taught him to let go of self-reliance and the dependence of past experiences to trust completely in God's provision. It was a humbling experience that reminded him of his frailty and the need to rely on God every step of his journey.

In our own lives, moments of God's silence can serve as a powerful reminder of our need for total reliance on Him. It is in these times that we are called to surrender our plans, our strengths, and our ambitions, and to trust wholeheartedly in God's wisdom and direction. As we learn to lean on Him completely, we discover the depth of His faithfulness and the sufficiency of His grace to sustain us through every trial and challenge.

As a Symbol of God's Diverse Ways.

God's silence in the desert indeed reflects His mysterious and diverse ways of working. It challenges human expectations and highlights the fact that God's voice is not always loud or overt, but can be subtle, yet impactful and transformative.

In Elijah's experience, the silence of God in the desert was a stark contrast to the dramatic displays of power witnessed on Mount Carmel. Instead of fire from heaven or mighty winds, Elijah encountered God in the stillness and quietness of the desert. This gentle whisper was a powerful reminder that God's ways are higher than our ways, and His thoughts are higher than our thoughts.

This moment serves as a testament of God's diverse ways of speaking and working in our lives. Sometimes He speaks through the loud and spectacular, but often He reveals Himself in the quiet and ordinary moments. It is in the silence that we are called to listen attentively, to discern His voice amidst the noise of the world, and to be open to the subtle nudges and whispers of His Spirit.

God's diverse ways of working also challenge us to let go of our preconceived notions and expectations of how He should act or speak. Instead, we are called to trust in His wisdom and sovereignty, knowing that He works all things together for our good.

This symbol of God's diverse ways encourages us to be open to His leading in all circumstances, whether in moments of silence or in times of loud proclamation. It reminds us that His voice can be found in the quiet places of our hearts, speaking words of comfort, guidance, and transformation. As we learn to listen and follow His lead, we discover the depth of His love and the richness of His presence in our lives.

Restoration and New Commission.

The period of silence led to Elijah's restoration and his new prophetic assignment. God provides sustenance, reassures Elijah, and gives him a renewed assignment. The period, therefore, becomes a pivotal moment in Elijah's ministry Journey.

Silence and the Prophetic Narrative.

Elijah's encounter with God's silence adds depth to his prophetic experience, highlighting that his journey includes times of profound revelation as well as moments of intimate communion with God.

In summary, Elijah's background has little or no recorded revelation prior to his emergence. God's silence on Elijah before and after his wilderness encounter serves purposes such as testing, transition, encouragement in solitude, teaching dependence, symbolising God's mysterious ways, and facilitating restoration and a renewed mandate. It adds depth to Elijah's prophetic experience.

Jeremiah's school of silence.

Expressing Lament and Despair.

Jeremiah expressed a deep lamentation and distress over the judgement pronounced on Judah. His cries and quest for understanding and guidance during the times of crisis reflect his anguish of experiencing God's apparent silence.

Testing of Faith.

The silence in Jeremiah's prophetic ministry served as a test of faith. Despite facing opposition and rejection, Jeremiah remains faithful to his calling, demonstrating perseverance in the midst of God's quietude.

Symbol of God's Sovereignty:

Jeremiah's experience of God's quietude underscores the sovereignty of God, highlighting that His ways and timings are beyond human understanding. This reaffirms Jeremiah's role as a messenger of God's will, despite the lack of direct communication.

Conveying Messages of Hope:

Despite the silence, Jeremiah delivers messages of hope and restoration. The silent season serves as a precursor to the eventual fulfilment of God's promise of a new covenant and the restoration of His people, as outlined in ***Jeremiah 31:31-34.***

Teaching Divine Lessons:

Jeremiah's life and ministry impart enduring lessons on the consequences of disobedience, the importance of repentance, and the eventual realisation of God's redemptive plan. His experiences serve as a testament to the faithfulness and justice of God.

The Struggle and Willful Surrender:

Jeremiah's encounter with God's silence reveals the human aspect of prophetic ministry. Despite facing rejection and personal struggles, he remains dedicated to conveying God's messages, demonstrating profound commitment to his divine calling.

A Test of Faith:

Jeremiah's experience of God's silence becomes a significant test of his faith. Amid turmoil and rejection, he continues to trust in God's promises and purpose, exemplifying unwavering faith in the face of adversity.

A Call to Repentance:

Through the silence, God calls His people, including Jeremiah, to repentance. The absence of direct communication serves as a reminder of the need for spiritual renewal and turning back to God, emphasising the importance of obedience.

A Message of Hope:

Despite the silence, there is a message of hope embedded within Jeremiah's experiences. It signifies that God is still at work, orchestrating events for the good of His people, even when He appears silent, instilling confidence in His faithfulness.

The Unfolding of God's Redemptive Plan:

Ultimately, God's silence in Jeremiah's life is part of the unfolding of His redemptive plan. It foreshadows the restoration and renewal that God promises to bring about, demonstrating His ultimate purpose for His people.

In summary, Jeremiah's encounter with God's silence encompasses a multifaceted journey of faith, repentance, sovereignty, hope, and the unfolding of God's redemptive purposes. It teaches us to trust in God's plan, even in silence, knowing that He is always working for our ultimate good and His glory.

Highlights.

Learning from Scripture.

Romans 15:4 and Hebrews 6:12 teach patience, comfort, and hope from past experiences.

Job's Turmoil and Faith.

Job's story reveals unwavering faith amidst suffering and God's apparent silence.

Honesty in Prayer.

Psalms demonstrate honesty with God about raw emotions and feelings.

Waiting on God's Faithfulness.

Psalm 40:1-3 emphasises waiting on God's faithfulness and shifting focus to Him.

God's Ever-Present Silence.

God's silence, seen in Psalms and Job experiences, doesn't mean absence.

Elijah's Desert Encounter.

Elijah's solitude in the desert reveals encounters with God's quiet voice.

Total Dependence on God.

Elijah learns absolute dependence on God's authority and provision.

Symbol of God's Diverse Ways.

God's silence reflects mysterious and transformative ways, as in Elijah's story.

Restoration and New Commission.

Elijah experiences restoration and a renewed prophetic assignment.

Expressing Lament and Despair.

Jeremiah's lamentation over Judah's judgement reveals anguish in God's silence.

Testing of Faith.

Jeremiah's faith is tested amidst rejection, demonstrating perseverance.

Symbol of God's Sovereignty.

God's silence symbolises His sovereignty beyond human comprehension.

Conveying Messages of Hope.

Jeremiah's silence precedes messages of hope and restoration.

Teaching Divine Lessons.

Jeremiah's ministry imparts lessons on repentance and God's redemptive plan.

Struggle and Willful Surrender.

Jeremiah's challenge with silence unveils the human aspect of prophetic dedication.

Chapter 6

Biblical Players

(Part II)

In this chapter, we delve deeper into the lives and experiences of individuals, families, and nations who traversed the valley of God's silence. These biblical narratives offer diverse insights and experiences to explore.

We begin by examining the Intertestamental period, a span of approximately 400 years characterized by the absence of prophetic voices and inspired writings. This era, known as the "Silent Years," follows the conclusion of the Old Testament prophets.

The last of these prophets, Malachi, completed his prophetic assignment around 400 BCE, marking the cessation of biblical prophetic utterances. Despite this silence, significant historical and political events unfolded during this time, including the reign of Alexander the Great and the rise of Hellenistic influence in the Middle East.

However, amidst these changes, there was a lack of divine revelation as the Old Testament scriptures were complete, and the New Testament had yet to be written. This period posed challenges for the Jewish community, including the encroachment of Hellenistic culture and religious persecution.

In the absence of canonical scriptures, other texts such as the Apocrypha and Pseudepigrapha emerged, offering insights into the religious and philosophical landscape of the time. While not universally accepted as inspired, these writings provide valuable context for understanding the religious and cultural developments during the Intertestamental period.

Expectation for the Messiah:

Despite the apparent silence of God, a palpable expectation for the arrival of the Messiah permeated Jewish communities during the Intertestamental period.

This fervent anticipation served as the backdrop for the emergence of Jesus as the long-awaited Messiah.

As the Intertestamental period draws to a close, events unfold leading to the birth of Jesus, marking a monumental transition in Christian history as the New Testament era dawns. While prophetic writings may have ceased, it is essential to recognize that God's presence remained steadfast throughout this period. Despite the absence of inspired scriptures, God's providence continued to shape the course of history, laying the groundwork for the unfolding narrative of redemption in the New Testament.

Biblical Examples of individual Players like.

Joseph.

Joseph's life journey in the Genesis account unfolds after this order.

Dreams and Family Turmoil Genesis 37.

Joseph's dreams of his future leadership assignment provoked jealousy and animosity among his brothers. Throughout the period, there was no explicit mention of God speaking or intervening.

Sold into Slavery-Genesis 37-39.

Out of jealousy, his brothers sold him into slavery, ending up in Egypt. While there, Joseph was falsely accused by his boss's wife, who made sexual advances towards him, resulting in his imprisonment, despite his faithfulness to Potiphar, his boss.

Interpreting Dreams in Prison Genesis 40.

While in prison, Joseph used his gift of interpreting dreams to help fellow inmates. However, there was no recorded direct communication from God to him during the period.

God's Intervention -Genesis 41.

In Genesis 41,God finally broke the silence in Joseph's favour. After interpreting Pharaoh's dreams accurately, he was elevated to a position of authority and influence. This marked a pivotal moment when God's plan for Joseph began to unfold visibly.

Joseph's life serves as a beacon of hope, showing us, God's silence is not His absence but a prelude to greater purposes. Just as Joseph's silent years led to his elevation and the fulfilment of God's plan, our season of waiting and silence can be a time of preparation for greater responsibilities ahead.

Joseph's prophetic journey from silence to God's intervention teaches us, it's not a season of abandonment. Instead, a period of refining, testing, and preparation for the remarkable roles He has destined for us. Like Joseph, may we trust in God's unfailing promises and remain steadfast in faith, knowing that He is always working behind the scenes for our good and the revelation of His glory.

Moses.

After fleeing the palace in Egypt, Moses spent years in the wilderness of Midian. During this period, viewed as quietude, Moses tended the sheep of his father-in-law, far from the glory of his previous life. Yet, it was in this period of silence that he was prepared for his divine assignment to lead the Israelites out of Egypt.

Moses' silent years in the desert of Midian teach us valuable lessons about God's timing, preparation, and faithfulness. It was in the quietness of the desert that Moses learned humility, dependence on God, and the importance of obedience.

This window in Moses' life was not a time wasted, but a season of preparation, shaping Moses into the leader and deliverer God intended him to be. It underscores the fact that God often works in silence, orchestrating events that refine the character of His chosen vessels in obscurity.

Like Moses, we may find ourselves in the place of apparent God's silence. These desert moments, though challenging, are often times for deep spiritual growth and preparation for the tasks ahead. It is in these silent seasons that God moulds our character, deepens our faith, and equips us for His purposes.

Moses' journey from the silence of the desert to the place of leading the Israelites out of Egypt serves as a powerful platform of God's faithfulness, provision, and transformative work in the lives of His people. It encourages us to trust in His timing and purpose, even when His voice seems silent, knowing that He is always at work for our good and unto His glory.

Esther.

Esther faced a critical moment of divine silentude in the land of Shushan as she prepared herself to approach King Xerxes to plead for the deliverance of her people. In the face of uncertainty and fear, Esther finds the courage to break the silence and speak up for her people. Despite the absence of explicit mention of God's direct communication or intervention during the time, she trusted in God's unseen hand guiding her actions.

Through her bravery and faith, she became an instrument of God's deliverance, ultimately leading to the preservation of the Jewish people. Her experience serves as a powerful reminder of God's providence and the importance of stepping out in faith, even in moments of apparent silence.

RUTH

Ruth's journey with her mother-in-law, Naomi, from Moab, the land where God was silent, to Bethlehem of Judea was marked by her silent acts of loyalty and devotion. In the fields of Boaz, Ruth silently gleaned grain to provide for their needs, showing her unwavering commitment to Naomi and their survival. Despite the absence of direct communication from God during this period, Ruth's faithfulness and humility spoke volumes. God's providence was evident in Ruth's quiet obedience and trust, leading to blessings beyond her imagination. Ruth's story teaches us about the power of silent faithfulness, the beauty of selfless love, and the assurance that God works behind the scenes to bring about His plans for our lives.

Exploring these characters and their circumstances, we glean from a window of God's silence, peering through obedience and patient waiting to honest lament and unwavering trust. Each experience enriches our understanding of how individuals go through these seasons and find meaning in their faith journeys.

Biblical Examples of Families who experienced God's silence.

Noah and his wife's experience during the time of the flood , offers a profound illustration of navigating God's silence.

As the story unfolds in Genesis, Noah receives clear and direct instructions from God to build an ark to save his family and pairs of animals from the impending Judgement. However, during the years of constructing the massive ark and preparing for the flood of Judgment, there was no record of God speaking directly to Noah or his wife. The extended period of silence could have been filled with doubts, questions, and uncertainties for Noah's family as they faced the heavy task ahead of them.

Despite the lack of direct communication, Noah and his wife remained faithful, obedient, and diligent in their work. They continued to follow the instructions given to them, trusting in the promise of God's deliverance even when His voice seemed distant. This silent season for Noah and his wife was a test of their faith, perseverance, and trust in God's plan. It required them to rely solely on the instructions they had received earlier and to remain steadfast in their commitment to follow through.

In the midst of the silence, Noah's family found strength in their unity, as they worked together to prepare for the flood. Their faithfulness and obedience were a testament to their unwavering trust in God's promises, even when His voice was not audible. Ultimately, God's faithfulness prevailed as the flood came, and Noah, his wife, their children, and the animals were safely carried through the waters in the ark. The silence they experienced was met with the fulfilment of God's plan for their deliverance and the preservation of life on earth.

Elkanah and Hannah

Hannah's experience in 1 Samuel illustrates the curse of infertility and the depth of her longing for a child. She prayed fervently at Shiloh, pouring out her soul before the Lord. Initially, Eli the priest misinterpreted her intense supplication, mistaking it for drunkenness. Despite her persistent prayers, there was a period of apparent silence from God.

However, when the time was right, God remembered Hannah's cries and granted her request with the birth of Samuel. This narrative reveals the power of persistent prayer and the faithfulness of God, even in times of silence.

The family of Elkanah and Hannah teaches us valuable lessons about the power of persistent prayer, the importance of trusting in God's timing, and the beauty of dedicating our children and all aspects of our lives to God's service. It also reminds us that God hears the cries of His people, even in the midst of silence, and He is faithful to fulfil His promises in His perfect time.

Zechariah and Elizabeth's story is a testament to God's faithfulness and the power of His timing. Despite being described as righteous and blameless, they faced the sorrow of infertility. However, God had a special plan for them.

While serving in the temple, Zechariah was visited by the angel Gabriel, who announced that Elizabeth would conceive and bear a son named John, who would prepare the way for the Messiah. Initially, Zechariah doubted the angel's message and was struck mute as a consequence. This period of silence became a time of reflection and deepening faith for Zechariah.

When John was born, Zechariah's speech was restored, leading to a profound declaration of praise and prophecy. Their story serves as a reminder that God's plans unfold in His perfect timing, often in ways we least expect. It teaches us to trust in God's promises and to be patient, knowing that He is always at work behind the scenes, orchestrating events for His glory.

Joseph and Mary.

The narrative of Joseph and Mary is a profound example of faith, obedience, and trust in God's plan, even in the face of uncertainty and silence. Mary, a virgin betrothed to Joseph, received the news from the angel Gabriel that she would conceive a son by the Holy Spirit, who would be named Jesus. This revelation brought awe and reverence, but also presented serious challenges, especially in the silence from God during this season of uncertainty.

Despite the confusion and societal implications, Mary chose to trust in God's plan. Joseph, too, faced a period of silence as he grappled with the news of Mary's pregnancy. It wasn't until an angel appeared to him in a dream that he understood God's purpose and took Mary as his wife. Their story teaches us the importance of surrendering to God's will, even in moments of confusion and uncertainty.

Their example of faith, obedience, and trust serves as a beacon of hope, urging us to place our trust in God's promises, even in the face of seemingly insurmountable challenges. Their journey reminds us that God's faithfulness to previous generations is a testament to His enduring love and provision for us today.

As we contemplate the journey of Joseph and Mary, may we draw courage from their unwavering faith in God's guidance, even amidst His apparent silence. Let us echo their resounding "yes" to God's will for our lives, finding solace in His assurances, and embracing His presence in every step of our journey. In doing so, may we discover peace and assurance, knowing that God is always by our side, leading us through the uncertainties of life with unfailing love and grace.

Biblical Examples of Nations who experienced God's silence.

Jerusalem.

Jerusalem, the heart of Israel and the centre of Jewish worship, experienced a profound silence during its destruction, as vividly depicted in the book of Lamentations. The prophet Jeremiah, often called the "weeping prophet," mourns the fall of the city and the devastation brought upon it by the Babylonian army. In the midst of this desolation, the people of Israel felt abandoned and alone, grappling with the stark reality of their beloved city being ravaged.

The silence of God during this dark period of Jerusalem's history was palpable. The once bustling city, renowned for its grandeur and significance in Jewish religious life, now lay in ruins. The temple, considered the sacred dwelling place of God on earth, was destroyed, adding to the sense of loss and abandonment felt by the people.

As Jeremiah laments the destruction of Jerusalem and the suffering of its inhabitants, his words echoed the profound grief and despair that enveloped the city. The silence of God seemed deafening amidst the cries of anguish and the ruins of what was once a flourishing centre of worship.

The destruction of Jerusalem serves as a poignant reminder of the consequences of disobedience and the severity of God's judgement. The silence of God during this period was a stark reflection of the broken covenant between Him and His people, as they faced the consequences of their sins and rebellion.

Despite the silence, however, there remained a glimmer of hope amidst the despair. Jeremiah's laments also spoke of a future restoration and renewal promised by God. The prophet foretold of a time when Jerusalem would be rebuilt, the temple restored, and the people of Israel reconciled with their God.

In this time of silence and desolation, the people of Israel were called to reflect on their sins, seek repentance, and turn back to God. The destruction of Jerusalem served as a powerful reminder of the importance of faithfulness, obedience, and reverence towards God's covenant.

The silence of God during the destruction of Jerusalem teaches us valuable lessons about the consequences of sin, the severity of God's judgement, and the enduring hope found in His promises of restoration and redemption. It calls us to examine our own lives, seek repentance, and turn to God in times of darkness and despair, knowing that His faithfulness endures even in the silence.

Nineveh.

The city of Nineveh, infamous for its wickedness, received a dire warning from the prophet Jonah about its impending destruction. Surprisingly, upon hearing Jonah's preaching, the people of Nineveh repented, and God relented from the disaster He had planned. However, after this remarkable display of repentance, there is no further mention of Nineveh turning back to God or receiving divine communication.

This apparent silence or lack of recorded divine intervention following Nineveh's repentance raises questions about the enduring impact of spiritual renewal and the continual need for seeking God's presence.

Egypt.

Egypt faced a series of devastating plagues sent by God through Moses to secure the release of the Israelites from slavery. These plagues served as a demonstration of God's power and judgement upon Egypt. Despite the magnitude of these events, there is no mention of direct communication between God and the Egyptian leaders during this time of upheaval. The silence from God during the plagues underscores the severity of His judgement and emphasises the need for Egypt to acknowledge His sovereignty. Nevertheless, even in the absence of direct communication, the plagues served as a clear message of God's power and the futility of opposing His will.

The Canaanite Nations.

The Canaanite nations inhabiting the Promised Land during the time of Joshua and the conquest of Canaan faced God's judgement through Israel. The conquest was marked by divine intervention, such as the falling of Jericho's walls. However, the Canaanite nations were not in direct communication with God and faced His judgement without clear dialogue or revelation.

This silence highlights the decisive actions of God through Israel as they fulfilled His commands to take possession of the Promised Land. The Canaanites faced the consequences of their disobedience and idolatry without direct interaction or warning from God.

The Philistines.

The Philistines were a recurring adversary of the Israelites during the time of the judges and kings.

They faced various defeats and setbacks, including the capture of the Ark of the Covenant. The Philistines witnessed God's power through the plagues that befell them due to their possession of the Ark.

However, there is no indication of direct communication or divine revelation to the Philistine leaders during these confrontations.
This silence underscores the divine judgment upon the Philistines for their defiance and the consequences of their actions, even in the absence of explicit communication from God.

Edom.

The nation of Edom, descendants of Esau, often clashed with the nation of Israel.

In the book of Obadiah, Edom is warned of impending judgement due to their mistreatment of Israel. However, there is no direct communication from God recorded regarding their fate.

The silence of God in Edom's history serves as a sobering reminder of the consequences of mistreating God's chosen people, leading to divine retribution without explicit dialogue.

Assyria.

Assyria, a powerful empire in ancient times, conquered the northern kingdom of Israel and threatened Judah with their cruelty and oppression.

The prophet Nahum pronounced judgment against Nineveh, the capital of Assyria, for its violence and wickedness.

The destruction of Nineveh eventually came, signifying God's judgement, but there is no recorded dialogue or interaction between God and the Assyrian leaders during this time.

The silence of God in Assyria's downfall emphasises the consequences of their actions and the fulfilment of prophetic warnings, showcasing God's sovereignty and justice.

The instances of God's silence with Jerusalem , Nineveh, Egypt, the Canaanite Nations, the Philistines, Edom, and Assyria illustrate the consequences of disobedience, idolatry, mistreatment of God's people, and wickedness. The absence of direct communication from God underscores His judgement upon nations that defy His commands and the fulfilment of prophetic warnings. It serves as a reminder of the significance of obedience and reverence toward God's sovereignty and His dealings with nations throughout history.

These examples from Scripture show us how individuals, families and nations encountered God's silence in different contexts, often as a result of their actions and inactions. The silentude served as a warning, a judgement, or a period of waiting for His purposes to unfold.

Summarising their similarities and significance.

All these nations encountered moments of God's silence as a consequence of their actions of rebellion, Which served various purposes, including warning of impending judgment, a period of waiting for repentance, or as a test of faith and dependence.

The historical narratives of nations and peoples in Scripture experiencing God's silence hold profound lessons for contemporary nations and societies:

Warning and Judgment.

The silence of God often serves as a warning sign of impending consequences for actions contrary to His will. It calls for introspection and repentance to avoid facing His judgments. Nations today can heed these warnings by aligning their policies and actions with principles of justice, righteousness, and compassion.

Repentance and Redemption:

Moments of God's silence can indeed serve as pivotal opportunities for repentance and redemption. Just as Nineveh responded to Jonah's warning with sincere repentance, individuals and nations facing God's apparent silence can choose to humble themselves, seek forgiveness, and realign with His covenant. God's mercy is abundant, and He is always ready to forgive those who earnestly seek Him with contrite hearts. These moments of silence can thus become catalysts for spiritual renewal and restoration, leading to a deeper relationship with God and a renewed commitment to His will.

Testing of Faith:

The silence of God can also be a test of faith and dependence on Him. It calls for steadfastness and firmness in His sovereignty, even in the midst of trials and uncertainties. Nations facing challenges can rely their faith in God's providence and guidance.

Divine Providence:

Despite the silence, God is always at work behind the scenes, orchestrating events for the fulfilment of His purposes. Trusting in His providence, even in moments of silence, leads to a deeper reliance on His faithfulness and goodness. Nations can trust in God's sovereignty over the affairs of the world, knowing that He works all things for the good of those who love Him.

Response to Warning Signs.

When faced with the silence of God, it is crucial for nations to respond with humility, repentance, and faith in God's integrity. It is a call to seek His face earnestly, to listen to the cries of the marginalised and oppressed, and to work towards justice and reconciliation. Nations that acknowledge their dependence on God and seek His guidance will find strength and wisdom in navigating the challenges of the times.

The lessons and instructions from the silence of God in Scripture offer timeless wisdom for nations today. By heeding these insights, nations can navigate the complexities of our world with faith, humility, and a commitment to righteousness and justice.

Highlights.

The Intertestamental Period:

The period of 400 years between Malachi and the New Testament is marked by a lack of prophetic voices and inspired writings.

Historical Shifts and Political Events:

Despite the silence, significant historical and political changes occurred, including Alexander the Great's reign and Hellenistic influence.

Absence of Divine Revelation:

With the completion of the Old Testament, there was a lack of inspired writings, signalling a period of God's apparent silence.

Challenges Faced by the Jewish Community:

During this time, challenges included the influence of Hellenistic culture and religious persecution.

Apocryphal and Pseudepigraphal Texts:

The Apocrypha and Pseudepigrapha offer insights into the religious and philosophical milieu of the Intertestamental window.

Expectation for the Messiah:

Despite God's silence, there was a fervent expectation for the arrival of the Messiah among Jewish communities.

Transition to the New Testament Era:

The period ends with events leading to the birth of Jesus, marking a significant shift in Christian history.

God's Continued Presence Despite Silence:

Despite the lack of prophetic voices, God's presence remained steadfast, shaping history for the New Testament narrative.

Joseph's Life Journey:

Dreams and Family Turmoil.
Joseph's dreams, betrayal by his brothers, slavery, and imprisonment marked a period of apparent silence from God.

Joseph's Interpretation of Dreams and God's Intervention:

In prison, Joseph interprets dreams, leading to his elevation by God's intervention after interpreting Pharaoh's dream.

Joseph's Silent Years as Preparation:

Joseph's silence teaches that God's silence is preparation for greater purposes ahead, culminating in his elevation.

Moses' Wilderness Experience:

Moses' silent years in Midian teach about God's timing, preparation, and faithfulness for his role in leading Israel.

Moses' Preparation in Silence:

In the desert, Moses learned humility, dependence on God, and obedience, preparing him for leadership.

Moses' Silent Period as Preparation:

Moses' silence highlights God's work in obscurity, preparing him to be the leader God intended.

Esther's Bravery in Silence:

Esther's courage in approaching King Xerxes, despite the perceived silence from God, which led to the preservation of her people.

Chapter 7

The Significance of God's Silence

In this chapter, we will be delving into the historical and contemporary context of events that have influenced individuals and societies. It prompts us to explore our past and present encounters, offering insight into our human experiences throughout time.

In our today's complex world, people across all spheres of human existence—such as the family, politics and governance, arts and entertainment, media, commerce and industry, religion or faith systems, etc.—encounter moments of God's quietude. These are times when efforts seem futile, and one feels the disconnect and distance from the creator of the universe.

The experiences within these pages reveal how God's plan unfolds over time, offering us the platform for personal and collective growth in the midst of life's challenges. The forces of perseverance, resilience, and transformative power contract during these silent seasons.

From the accounts of history to modern-day narratives, we glean insights into the multifaceted nature of God's quietude and the coping strategies necessary for navigating such seasons. As we examine historical records and contemporary stories, we uncover the varied ways in which individuals and communities have grappled with God's silence. Through the exploration, we discern the resilience, faith, and perseverance required to endure and thrive amidst moments of God's quietude. By learning from the experiences of others, we gain valuable perspectives and strategies for finding peace, purpose, and hope in the midst of uncertainty and apparent silence from God.

Personal Testimonies of Faith:

Individuals share their faith experiences of how they dealt with moments of God's quietude, finding strength in God and His ways. These testimonies highlight deep spiritual growth and maturity.

Reflections on Covenant Promises:

Engaging God's acts of faithfulness in the past, his covenant promises in Scripture and in contemporary times, help shape one's complete reliance on Him during silent seasons.

Character Refinement Through Challenges:

The silent seasons in family narratives often lead to character refinement and spiritual growth, a more united front illustrating God's transformative work.

Spiritual Quests for Understanding:

Delving into historical and contemporary encounters with God's silence stirs up inner quests for deeper spiritual understanding and connectivity.

Resilience Amidst Tough Moments:

Drawing on the track record of God's past interventions and faithfulness equips individuals with resilience to cope during life's toughest moments.

Navigating Silence with Guidance:

The spiritual essence of family narratives offers guidance for navigating silent seasons, providing insights and coping strategies.

Reliance on God's Unchanging Character.

Through reflections on Scripture and personal testimonies, individuals learn to rely on God's unchanging character during times of silence.

Transformation Through Faith Journeys:

Family narratives that illuminate the transformative power of faith journeys, showcasing how God's silence leads to spiritual growth and maturity.

Deepening Connection with God:

The silence season becomes an opportunity to deepen one's connection with God, fostering intimacy and trust in His plan.

Discovering Strength in Vulnerability.

Embracing vulnerability during silent seasons reveals hidden strength and resilience, leading to personal and spiritual growth.

Faithfulness Amidst Uncertainty.

The silent seasons in the family experience highlight one's faithfulness even in the midst of uncertainty and challenges, inspiring hope.

Revelations Through Quiet Contemplation:

Quiet moments of contemplation during silent seasons often lead to profound revelations and spiritual insights.

Resting in God's Sovereignty:

Trusting in God's sovereignty becomes a cornerstone during silent seasons, offering peace and assurance in the midst of uncertainty.

Embracing the Mystery of God's Timing:

The silence season teaches individuals to embrace the mystery of God's timing, learning patience and endurance.

Renewed Faith Through Shared Experiences:

Sharing family narratives of God's faithfulness during silent seasons renews faith and inspires wisdom in others on their own spiritual journey. Coping with God's silence at a national level requires a multifaceted approach that encompasses spiritual, emotional, social, and cultural dimensions.

By fostering unity, empathy, and resilience, a nation can navigate the challenges of uncertainty with a sense of purpose and collective strength. These coping strategies aim to provide support and guidance for individuals and communities as they navigate their spiritual journeys during times of perceived God's silence.

Reflections on Israel's History and Contemporary Parallels.

The historical narratives of Israel's almost 430 years in Egyptian bondage and 70 years of Babylonian captivity, Exemplifies God's silence at national level. These narratives, although being ancient, yet offer timeless insights into human actions, divine timing, and God's all-encompassing plan.

The extended period of slavery endured by the Israelites in Egypt raises serious questions about the why of God's distance or disconnect in the face of oppression. Despite their groanings by reason of the bondage and fervent cries for deliverance, the initial lack of intervention seems perplexing and mind-boggling. Where is the God of Abraham, Isaac and Jacob, the omnipotent, the omnipresent, the Omniscient and Omnibenevolent one ?

However, the accounts reveal that God's silence is never an abandonment but rather a part of His bigger plan. The eventual deliverance under the leadership of Moses explains the significance of God's timing and faithfulness towards His promises and detailed plan.

Furthermore, the Babylonian captivity, which was a consequence of idolatry and gross disobedience, offers fuller insight into God's quietude.

Let it be known that, within this context, it served as judgement, with the promise of restoration and eventual return to their homeland, emphasising repentance as key, highlighting His silence is not eternal but a purpose in his all-encompassing plan of redemption.

Contemporary Insights for Reflection.

These historical narratives are not mere accounts of the past; but resonate with contemporary parallels across various spheres of human experience.

Personal Trials and Challenges:

In the midst of personal trials and challenges, individuals have grappled with the perceived absence of God's voice and intervention. This silence becomes a testing ground, sparking self-examination and a quest for meaning and understanding.

The Impact of the COVID-19 Pandemic:

The COVID-19 pandemic has been a time of global upheaval, causing many to feel as though God is silent amidst the chaos and suffering. The loss of lives, societal turmoil, and uncertainty have led people to question why God seems silent in the face of such devastation. This has prompted individuals to seek divine understanding and guidance, turning to prayer, reflection, and scriptural practices to find solace and meaning in the midst of the crisis. While the silence of God during such challenging times may be difficult to comprehend, it is important to remember that God's ways are higher than our ways, and His timing is not always our own. In times of crisis, it is crucial to lean on faith, trusting that God is present even in the silence and that He is working out His purposes for the ultimate good of humanity.

Through prayer, faith, and community support, individuals can find strength, hope, and resilience to navigate through the darkness of uncertainty and emerge stronger on the other side.

Environmental Crises:

The escalating environmental crises of today's world, from climate change to deforestation, resonates with God's silence. Mankind faces the consequences of ecological meltdown and devastation, questioning the role of God's intervention in the midst of the environmental peril. This silent narrative reminds us of our responsibility of managing the planet and the need for divine insight in the midst of the ecological upheavals.

The Spiritual Dryness in Modern Times:

The contemporary spiritual landscapes reveal seasons of spiritual dryness, where the absence of God's presence and His kingdom values are acutely felt. These periods become crucibles for testing and growth, urging us to persevere in faith despite the apparent solemnity.

Whether in ancient times or the modern era, faith has always been an anchor. Engaging scripture feeds our faith and serves as the navigator's light for the journey. The accounts of Israel's history remind us that just as God intervened in the past and led His people through periods of silence and gave them inheritance, He remains the same even today.

For I am the Lord, I do not change; Therefore you are not consumed, O sons of Jacob. Malachi 3:6.

In summary, the clouds of God's silence have been seen across the sky for ages, signalling judgments, global purging, redemption, and the rhythmic dance between God's timing and human responsibility. As we navigate personal silent seasons, may we find solace in God's attributes, comfort in the person of the Holy Spirit, and an unwavering hope in the promises of a covenant keeping God who is ever present in moments of silence, leading us towards purpose. Looking unto Jesus, the author and finisher of our faith.

Highlights:

Personal Testimonies of Faith:

Sharing experiences of challenges, strength in God, and spiritual growth.

Reflections on Covenant Promises:

Engaging with God's past faithfulness and promises in Scripture.

Character Refinement Through Challenges:

Silent seasons leading to character growth, showing God's work.

Spiritual Quests for Understanding:

Exploring historical and contemporary encounters with God's silence.

Resilience Amidst Tough Moments:

Drawing on past faithfulness to cope in life's toughest times.

Navigating Silence with Guidance:

Family narratives offering insights and coping strategies.

Reliance on God's Unchanging Promises:

Learning to trust God's promises during silent seasons.

Transformation Through Faith Journeys:

Growth and maturity through faith, despite silent times.

Deepening Connectivity with God:

Using silence to foster intimacy and trust in God's plan.

Discovering Strength in Vulnerability:

Finding hidden strength and resilience during silent seasons.

Faithfulness Amidst Uncertainty:

Demonstrating faithfulness even in uncertain, silent times.

Revelations Through Quiet Contemplation:

Profound insights and spiritual revelations in quiet moments.

Resting in God's Sovereignty:

Trusting in God's sovereignty for peace and assurance.

Embracing the Mystery of God's Timing:

Learning patience and endurance through understanding God's timing.

Personal Trials and Challenges:

Testing ground prompting self-examination and quest for understanding.

Impact of COVID-19 Pandemic:

Global crisis leading to seeking divine guidance amidst turmoil.

Environmental Crises:

Consequences of ecological degradation questioning divine intervention.

Spiritual Dryness in Modern Times:
Seasons of spiritual dryness urging perseverance in faith.

Chapter 8

The Transformative Power of Divine Revelation

This chapter begins with the definition of terms captured, to shed more light and provide fuller insight into the subject of our deliberations.

TRANSFORMATION:

Refers to a fundamental change or alteration in form, nature, character, or structure. It involves the process of complete or significant change, resulting in a new state or condition that differs significantly from the original. In a personal or spiritual context, transformation refers to a deep and lasting change in beliefs, attitudes, behaviours, or perspectives, leading to a more evolved, enlightened, or spiritually aligned way of being.

TRANSFORMATIVE POWER:

Denotes the capacity to create a fundamental shift in someone or something, leading to a notable and positive difference in their nature, character, or circumstances. This term is used to describe the profound impact that an event, experience, or influence can have on a person's life, beliefs, behaviours, or outlook.

DIVINE REVELATION:

Refers to the disclosure or unveiling of mysteries, spiritual insights, truths, or messages that are far more higher and superior for human capacity to know or understand.

This is a direct communication from God to the hearts of individuals, Ways the power of God's revelation is seen throughout the scriptures and in the lives of individuals, families, churches and nations.

The Revelation of God's Character & Ways:

Divine revelation unveils the character and ways of God to humanity. Through encounters like Moses' experience at the burning bush in Exodus 3, Isaiah's vision of God's glory in Isaiah 6, and John's revelation on the island of Patmos in Revelation 1, we gain insights into the holiness, love, sovereignty, and majesty of God.

The Revelation of God's Will:

Divine revelation unravels God's will and purposes. In the Old Testament, prophets received messages from God to guide the people of Israel. For example, the prophecies of Isaiah, Jeremiah, and Ezekiel conveyed God's warnings, promises, and plans for His people.

The Revelation of Redemption:

The Bible reveals God's redemptive plan for humanity through divine revelation. The birth, life, death, and resurrection of Jesus Christ were all foretold in the Scriptures by divine revelation. This ultimate act of redemption was communicated through the prophets and later through the apostles.

The Inspired Scriptures:

The Bible itself is a product of divine revelation. The authors of the Scriptures were inspired by God to inscribe. 2 Timothy 3:16 states, "All Scripture is God breath and profitable for teaching, for reproof, for correction, and for training in righteousness.

Personal Encounters:

Throughout the Bible, individuals had personal encounters with God that transformed and deliberately changed their lives. Examples include Jacob wrestling with God in Genesis 32, Saul's conversion on the road to Damascus in Acts 9, and Peter's vision regarding the inclusion of the Gentiles in God's salvation plan. Acts 10.

Guidance and Direction:

Divine revelation provides guidance and direction. In times of uncertainty or decision-making, seeking God's guidance through prayer and meditation on His Word can provoke divine insights and clarity.

Empowerment for the Ministry:

Divine revelation equips the called, for the work of ministry and service. The Holy Spirit, indwells the believer, provides the spiritual enabling to fulfill God's purposes on earth.

Confirmation of Truth:

Divine revelation confirms the truth of God's promises. Throughout history, God has fulfilled prophecies ,made true His promises, validating His Word and reinforcing the faith of believers.

Scriptural Encounters Exemplifying the Transformative power of God's revelation:

Paul's Conversion on the Damascus Road:
Acts 9:1-19 illuminates

Saul, once a persecutor of early Christians, had a life-altering encounter with the Lord Jesus on the road to Damascus, where he was enveloped in a blinding light. In this encounter, he hears the voice of Jesus, questioning, "Saul, Saul, why are you persecuting me?" This transformative encounter led to Saul's conversion to the Christian faith, prompting his redefinition as Paul, the Apostle of Jesus Christ. His journey unfolds to make him one of the foremost Apostles in Christian history, shaping the trajectory of the faith and influencing countless believers through his teachings and writings.

Moses at the Burning Bush referencing Exodus 3:1-14:

In the solitude of the desert, Moses encounters a remarkable sight: a burning bush that remains unconsumed by the flames. From within this extraordinary phenomenon, God manifests His holy presence and commissions Moses to lead the Israelites out of bondage in Egypt. This profound revelation transforms Moses from a mere shepherd into a chosen instrument of God—a deliverer and leader tasked with guiding His people towards their purpose and prophetic inheritance.

The Transfiguration of Jesus according to Matthew 17:1-8:

Peter, James, and John were privileged to witness the transfiguration of Jesus on a high mountain, where Jesus' appearance was transformed, and His face shone like the sun, while His clothes became as white as light. This extraordinary event affirmed Jesus' divine nature and His role as the Son of God.

Daniel's Vision of the Four Beasts in Daniel 7:1-28:

Daniel had a vision of four great beasts rising out of the sea, symbolising powerful kingdoms. In his vision, he saw one like a Son of Man coming in the clouds of heaven, with dominion and glory.

This revelation gave Daniel insight into the future kingdoms and the ultimate triumph of God's kingdom. It transformed Daniel's understanding of history and God's plan for the world.

The Road to Emmaus in the accounts of Luke 24:13-35:

Two disciples namely, Luke and Cleopas were walking to Emmaus, saddened by Jesus' crucifixion and death.

Jesus appears to them, but they did not recognize Him at first.
As they walked, Jesus explained the Scriptures to them, revealing how the Messiah had to suffer and rise again. When Jesus broke bread with them, their eyes were opened, and they recognized Him.

This revelation transformed their grief into joy and ignited a burning faith in their hearts.

The Vision of Ezekiel's Dry Bones referencing Ezekiel 37:1-14:

Ezekiel saw a vision of a valley full of dry bones, symbolising the hopeless state of Israel. God asked Ezekiel if the bones could live again, and Ezekiel responded only God knew. God commanded Ezekiel to prophesy to the bones, and they came back to life, forming a vast army.

This revelation symbolised God's power to restore and revive His people, even in the midst of despair.

It transformed Ezekiel's understanding of God's ability to bring new life and hope to His people.

Peter:

In Matthew 16:13-20, Peter receives divine intelligence about Jesus Christ' identity and mission. This revelation did not just affirm Peter's faith but also gave him insight into the messiahship and sonship of Christ. It marked a turning point in understanding his role as a disciple and future leader in the early church.

Mary Magdalene:

After witnessing the resurrection of Jesus, Mary Magdalene received a deep revelation when she encountered the resurrected Jesus at the empty tomb in John 20:11-18. The encounter transformed her from a grieving disciple into a bold Evangelist, preaching Christ' resurrection.

These biblical encounters unfold the impact of God's revelation in the lives of individuals and communities. They show how encountering God's presence, voice, and purpose can transform people, redirect their paths, strengthen their faith, and bring about a renewed hope.

The transformative power of God's revelation is more than head knowledge; but a revealed word with the power to shift our understanding, identity, and purpose. By encountering these truths, people have been led into a deeper relationship with God.

The scenery of Mount Sinai, where Moses received the Ten Commandments from God, stands as a vivid illustration of divine revelation. In Exodus 19-20, amidst thunder, lightning, and the sound of a trumpet, God imparts the commandments to Moses, to shape the moral conduct and deepen covenant relationship with the children of Israel. This pivotal moment solidifies the foundation of Israel's faith and underscores the importance of obedience to God's laws in their communal life.

Similarly, the teachings of Jesus Christ in the Gospels are revelations of the mysteries of God and His kingdom. These revelations penetrate beyond mere intellectual understanding, reaching into the depths of the heart and resulting in significant spiritual transformation.

Throughout history, God's revelation has left an indelible impact on societies and cultures. The prophets of old, such as Isaiah, Jeremiah, and Ezekiel, delivered messages of divine judgment and hope to the nation of Israel, calling its people to repentance and faithfulness to God's covenant.

The transformative power of divine revelation in scripture is multifaceted and far-reaching. It shapes individual lives, communities, and civilizations, leading to a deeper understanding of God's purposes and a faithful response to His call. As believers engage in prayer, fasting, and the study of God's word, they are continually transformed into the likeness of Christ, empowered to bear witness of His truth and love.

In the journey of faith, the mysterious nature of silence plays an integral role, challenging us to deepen our relationship with God, discern His purposes in moments of perceived silence. This journey of intimacy with God strengthens our faith, fosters trust, and ultimately leads to a deeper understanding of His sovereign will and plan for each believer's life.

Principles of Navigating God's Silence.

God's Silence as part of the Journey:

Recognize that God's silence is a natural facet of the spiritual journey of destiny, and doesn't necessarily indicate abandonment.

The Practice of Patience:

During this season, patience is a key component. Understanding that the timing of answers to prayers may not align with your expectations. Continue to seek and trust in the process.

Reflect on Your Spiritual Path:

Use the season for self examination and evolve to a better version of yourself looking unto Jesus. Reflect on your relationship with God, your mandate, and faith walk.

Maintaining the prayer culture:

Remaining prayerful and consistent in fulfilling one's kingdom assignment is indeed crucial, especially during moments of God's apparent silence. Persistence in prayer, studying the Word, and engaging in acts of kindness can help strengthen spiritual connectivity and deepen one's relationship with God.

Godly and Experienced Mentors:

Seeking the counsel of mentors who have experienced transformation through encounters with God's solitude is indeed a valuable asset. Mentors can offer fresh insights and perspectives, guiding individuals through seasons of silence and helping them discern God's will more clearly. Their wisdom and experience can provide the much-needed encouragement and direction during times of uncertainty.

Accept the Process:

God's silence can indeed serve as a test of faith and a pathway to spiritual maturation. Trusting that there is a purpose behind it, even when it's not clear at the time, allows us to lean on His wisdom and sovereignty. Embracing this perspective can deepen our trust in God's plan and ultimately lead to growth and maturity in our spiritual experience.

Let Go of Preconceived Expectations:

Letting go of all preconceived notions and being open to receiving answers in unexpected ways is essential for embracing God's guidance and wisdom. Sometimes, His messages come to us in ways we least expect, so maintaining an open mind and heart allows us to recognize His presence and direction, even in the midst of silence.

Focus on Actions:

Living out our faith while waiting for God's instructions is crucial. One way to do this is by practising kindness, not only to those in material need but also to those who may be spiritually impoverished. By extending compassion and generosity in both aspects, we align ourselves with God's heart for humanity and demonstrate our faith in action.

In the midst of God's voice, His silence becomes a personal experience—a journey whose path leads to a significant understanding of our faith and a stronger connection with God when the silence is eventually broken.

During those moments, we are called to trust in His sovereignty, even when we cannot hear His voice or discern His presence. It challenges us to rely on the revelation we possess about God's character, and promises, even in the absence of immediate answers or clear direction.

When God breaks the silence, it's a moment of revelation and clarity. We gain new insights, understanding, and a deeper intimacy with Him as we reflect on the lessons learned during the period.

As we journey through the maze of God's silence and moments of divine revelation, we are shaped and refined, emerging as individuals of deeper faith, resilience, and strength. Learning to walk by faith, even when we cannot see, we place our trust in the God who speaks through His silence, guiding us with steadfast love and wisdom.

Revelation holds transformative power, evident in the experiences of biblical figures like Isaiah and John. Isaiah's encounter with God compelled him to respond, "Here am I. Send me!" (Isaiah 6:8), while John's visions on Patmos provided profound insights recorded in the Book of Revelation. These encounters not only conveyed divine messages but also prepared these individuals for their unique divine purposes.

Hebrews 13:5 offers profound comfort: "I will never leave you nor forsake you." This promise becomes a beacon of hope for individuals navigating uncertainties and enduring periods of apparent silence, serving as a steadfast reminder of God's unwavering support.

Similarly, Deuteronomy 31:6 reveals a resolute stance: "Be strong and courageous. Do not be afraid or terrified because of them, for the Lord your God goes with you; he will never leave you nor forsake you." These words of encouragement serve as a powerful declaration, reinforcing the enduring presence of God even in the face of challenges and trials.

Psalm 114:1-5 stands as a sharp reminder of God's unfailing presence with Judah, even during times of apparent silence. This scripture reassures believers that God's presence remains constant and steadfast, regardless of the challenges and circumstances they may encounter.

Highlights.

Transformation Definition:

A fundamental change or alteration in form, nature, character, or structure, often leading to a new state significantly different from the original.

Transformative Power:

The ability to create a profound shift in someone or something, resulting in notable and positive changes.

Divine Revelation:

The disclosure of spiritual insights, truths, or messages beyond human understanding, often considered direct communication from God.

Transformative Power of Divine Revelation:

Creating significant, lasting change through divine insight, resulting in shifts in perspectives, behaviours, beliefs, and outcomes.

Impact of Divine Revelation:

Deep influence on individuals, communities, and history, revealing God's will, truths, and purposes through various forms such as visions, dreams, and inspired writings.

Revelation of God's Character:

Unveiling of God's attributes and holiness through encounters like Moses' burning bush and Isaiah's vision.

Revelation of God's Will:

Providing clarity on God's purposes, as seen through the prophecies of Isaiah, Jeremiah, and Ezekiel.

Revelation of Redemption:

Unfolding of God's redemptive plan, fulfilled through the birth, life, death, and resurrection of Jesus Christ.

The Inspired Scriptures:

The Bible as a product of divine revelation, guiding believers and providing wisdom.

Personal Encounters:

Transformational experiences with God, as seen in Jacob's wrestling, Saul's conversion, and Peter's vision.

Guidance and Direction:

Offering clarity and insight, aiding decision-making and spiritual growth.

Empowerment for the Ministry:

Equipping believers with wisdom, discernment, and spiritual gifts for service.

Confirmation of Truth:

Fulfilment of prophecies and promises, validating God's Word throughout history.

Transformation and Renewal:

The power of divine revelation to transform lives and renew minds, leading to personal growth.

Navigating Divine Silence:

Understanding God's silence as part of the spiritual experience, cultivating and activating patience, prayer, seeking counsel, focusing on actions of faith, and trusting in God's sovereignty.

Chapter 9

Obedience and Yieldedness to God's Will

The Greek term "hypakoe" points to obedience, meaning to listen and submit to authority or instruction. It involves the readiness to follow commands or instructions. On the other hand, there isn't a direct Greek word for "yieldedness."

The term "paradosi" suggests surrender or yielding, conveying the idea of handing oneself over or giving in, depending on the context.

Obedience and complete surrender to God's will are fundamental requirements in the kingdom of God. Scripture consistently reveals the significance of a surrendered life. Throughout the New Testament, especially in the Gospels, Jesus' life and ministry depicts complete surrender to the fathers will.

Jesus The Patterned Son.

His Incarnation.

Jesus' willingness to incarnate was in perfect alignment with the Father's will for His life. Mary's response in Luke 1:38 exemplifies her submission to God's plan, paving the way for Jesus to enter the world as the Son of God. Throughout His earthly ministry, Jesus demonstrated unflinching obedience to the Father's will, fulfilling His divine assignment with humility and selflessness. This act of obedience ultimately led to the redemption of humanity, as Jesus sacrificially gave His life to reconcile humanity back to God.

The Father's Business

From an early age, Jesus displayed profound obedience to the Father's will. In Luke 2:49, when Mary and Joseph found Him in the temple, His response revealed His commitment to fulfilling God's purpose for His life.

Jesus recognized the urgency of His mission and prioritized His Father's business above all else. This early dedication and commitment to obedience foreshadowed His lifelong dedication to carrying out the Father's will, serving as a model of submission for believers throughout the ages.

Jesus' Baptism and Heaven's Approval.

Jesus' baptism by John marked a significant moment of obedience to God's plan. As recorded in Matthew 3:13-17, His submission to baptism demonstrated His commitment to fulfilling all righteousness. The divine affirmation that followed, with God declaring, "This is my beloved Son, in whom I am well pleased," underscored the depth of Jesus' obedience and pleased the Father's heart. This public declaration signaled the beginning of Jesus' earthly ministry and affirmed His role as the beloved Son who obediently walked in accordance with the Father's will.

Jesus was Tempted in Every Way.

After His baptism, Jesus encounters a period of testing in the wilderness, as recounted in Matthew 4:1-11. Despite facing intense temptation from the devil backed by His entire kingdom, Jesus exemplified absolute obedience to God's Word. With each temptation, He countered the adversary's schemes with the authority of Scripture, declaring, "Be gone, Satan! For it is written, 'You shall worship the Lord your God and him only shall you serve.'" This pivotal moment underscores Jesus' steadfast commitment to aligning His actions with the will of the Father, demonstrating the power of obedience in overcoming temptation and fulfilling God's purposes.

Jesus lived the Father's Will.

Throughout His life and ministry, Jesus exemplified total obedience to the Father's will. In John 5:30, He unequivocally stated, "I can do nothing on my own. As I hear, I judge, and my judgement is just, because I seek not my own will but the will of him who sent me." This profound declaration encapsulates Jesus' commitment to aligning His actions and decisions with the divine purpose entrusted to Him by the Father. By strategically prioritising the Father's will above His own desires, Jesus set a powerful example of obedience for His followers, emphasising the importance of seeking and fulfilling God's will in all aspects of life.

Humility in Service:

Another facet of Jesus' obedience is exemplified in His humility. In Philippians 2:5-8, Paul provides a detailed narrative of Jesus' humility, often described as the kenosis experience. Jesus willingly relinquished His heavenly glory to take on the role of a servant and was obedient to the point of death, even death on a cross. This profound act of humility and obedience demonstrates Jesus' complete submission to the Father's will and His willingness to sacrifice Himself for the redemption of humanity. It serves as a powerful example for believers to emulate, reminding us of the importance of humility and obedience in our own lives.

Suffering in Obedience on the Cross:

The apex of His obedience was manifested on the cross. In the Garden of Gethsemane, He fervently prayed, "My Father, if it is possible, let this cup pass from me; nevertheless, not as I will, but as you will" -Matthew 26:39. Jesus' supreme act of submission was evident in His readiness to endure the cross for the redemption of humanity.

Apostle Paul experience.

In Galatians 2:20, Paul articulates the essence of a surrendered life with profound clarity:

"I have been crucified with Christ; it is no longer I who live, but Christ lives in me; and the life which I now live in the flesh I live by faith in the Son of God, who loved me and gave Himself for me."

This verse encapsulates the transformative power of embracing the crucifixion of the self and allowing Christ to find embodiment in us. It signifies a radical shift from self-centred living to a life guided by faith in the sacrificial love of Jesus Christ. Paul's words echo the profound truth that true life is found in surrendering to Christ, allowing His presence to permeate every aspect of our being, guiding our actions and decisions.

KEY POINTS TO ILLUMINATE THIS TRUTH.

To be Crucified with Christ.

This concept conveys the idea of the believer identifying with Christ in his life and death. Signifying a deep change and transformation in the life of the believer.

An end to the old way of life marked by sin and selfishness. Signifying putting to death the old lifestyle.

Just as Christ died on the cross for the sins of mankind, believers know that their old sinful nature was crucified with Christ. Signifying an end to the dominion of sin in their lives.

Conveying the promise of a new life. As Christ was raised back from the dead, believers in like manner are also raised through the mystery of baptism to the newness of life. Romans 6:4.

Speaks to the believer's new identity. They are no longer defined by their past identity or sins but are now identified with Christ in His death, burial, and resurrection. Through faith in Jesus Christ, believers are united with Him in His death, symbolised by baptism, and raised to new life, empowered by His resurrection. This transformation brings about a new identity characterised by forgiveness, redemption, and righteousness, enabling believers to live victoriously and walk in the freedom and power of Christ.

Enables the believer to live a life of faith, empowered by the Holy Spirit.

In essence, to be crucified with Christ is foundational to our Christian experience. It signifies death to our old self, our sinful nature, and our former way of life. This act of crucifixion symbolises our identification with Christ in His death on the cross, where our sins were atoned for and we were set free from the power of sin and death. Through this crucifixion with Christ, we die to ourselves and our selfish desires, allowing Christ to live in and through us, empowering us to live a life that is pleasing to God and characterised by love, obedience, and holiness.

CHRIST LIVES IN ME.

Once a believer identifies with Christ, their life is no longer their own but belongs to Christ and His kingdom agenda. This means living in accordance with His teachings, values, and priorities. The believer's life is now characterised by a pursuit of righteousness, love, and service to others, guided by the Holy Spirit who dwells within them.

The Holy Spirit plays a crucial role in enabling believers to live out the fullness of Christ in their lives. Through the indwelling presence of the Holy Spirit, believers are empowered to bear fruit, grow in spiritual maturity, and walk in obedience to God's will. The Spirit enables believers to live transformed lives, reflecting the character of Christ and making a meaningful impact in the world around them.

Living by Faith.

Living by faith is indeed a hallmark of the believer's life. It involves trusting in Jesus Christ as the source of guidance, purpose, and strength in every aspect of life. This reliance on Christ enables believers to navigate challenges, make decisions, and fulfil their calling with confidence and assurance.

Central to the believer's life is the love of Christ, exemplified by His sacrificial death on the cross. This sacrificial love serves as the foundation of the believer's new life in Christ and motivates them to live a life of love and selflessness towards others. As believers grow in their understanding of Christ's love, they are empowered to sacrificially serve others, demonstrating the transformative power of the gospel in their lives.

Apostle Paul's conversion and yieldedness exemplifies a dramatic transformation from being a persecutor of Christians to an Apostle of Jesus Christ by the will of God.

In Acts 9, his encounter with Jesus on the road to Damascus led to his humble request, What shall I do, Lord? He lived in obedience to the heavenly vision.

Jesus assigned him a ministry marked by obedience. He wrote in Galatians 1:15-16, "But when it pleased God, who separated me from my mother's womb and called me through His grace, to reveal His Son in me, that I might preach Him among the Gentiles, I did not immediately confer with flesh and blood.

Paul devoted his entire life to this assignment, spreading the Gospel of the kingdom of God and planting churches, regardless of the hardships he faced. His obedience led him to endure immense suffering for the sake of the Gospel. In 2 Corinthians 11:23-28, he recounts the trials he faced, including beatings, imprisonments, and shipwrecks. Yet, through it all, he remained faithful to his calling and steadfast in his faith.

The lives of Jesus and Paul reveal significant obedience, yieldedness, and faithfulness to God. Their examples challenge and inspire believers to follow in their footsteps, surrendering their wills to God's perfect plan, and serving faithfully in all circumstances.

As part of one's earthly experience, we encounter seasons where God's voice or intervention is purposefully withheld. During these times, the call to the Father's will beckons us not just to follow explicit directions or hidden signals but to the very character of God.

The path of obedience, especially during seasons of God's quietude, serves as a mark of steadfast faith. Abraham's test of faith to sacrifice his son Isaac becomes a practical example of steadfast faith even when clear guidance appeared absent. He trusted in God's plan in the midst of uncertainty, revealing his readiness to obey.

Similarly, Job's surrender to God's will amidst immense trials. Enduring unimaginable suffering, including the loss of family, wealth, and health, Job's steadfast faith was demonstrated through his willingness to accept and submit to God's plan.

His response to God's silent moments reveals remarkable resilience and trust in His sovereignty, even without His immediate response. His words were, "The Lord gives and the Lord takes away; blessed be the name of the Lord" Job 1:21. signifying his acceptance of the Father's will even in challenging times.

Throughout scripture, obedience and reliance on God's integrity and ability reverberates, especially during tough seasons marked by His apparent disconnect. Trusting Him means surrendering to His plan and will, even when His voice seems distant.

Job exemplifies a complete surrendered life, declaring, "Though he slay me, yet will I hope in him" Job 13:15, in the midst of suffering and God's apparent silence. Job's undivided devotion depicts total surrender and yieldedness, acknowledging God's sovereignty over his life. The silence sometimes is to test genuine yieldedness and challenge the extent to which one can go for him. Job's example stands as a timeless guide to our response to God's silence. The question still stands, is one willing to yield to the fathers will, even when circumstances are adverse ? Are we willing to tow the path of the fathers instructions no matter the cost?

God's covenant system of obedience and yieldedness as a lifestyle, are key requirements before, during and after His seasons of quietness. It encourages trust in God's plans, even when they surpass one's immediate understanding, and yields with the knowledge that He rules in the affairs of mankind.

Moses, leading the Israelites through the wilderness, embodies obedience and yieldedness in the midst of the silent period. Despite not always receiving clear instructions, he humbly followed God by observing the pillar of cloud during the day and the pillar of fire during the night.

David in the Psalms surrendered to God's will during periods of apparent silence revealing his yielded spirit. Psalm 27:14 encourages patiently waiting on the Lord, reflecting a posture of obedience and trust in God's timing.

These examples are testaments of hope, illustrating true obedience goes beyond audible instructions, relying on yielded hearts and unwavering trust, especially when God's voice seems distant.

Highlights.

Obedience and Yieldedness Defined:

"Hypakoe" in Greek means obedience, listening, and submitting to authority or instruction.

"Paradosi" : suggests surrender or yielding, conveying the idea of handing oneself over or giving in, depending on the context.

Fundamental Requirements in the Kingdom:

Obedience and complete surrender to God's will.
Scripture reveals the significance of a surrendered life.

Jesus Christ the Patterned Son.

Incarnation:

Jesus accepted His incarnation, lived according to the Father's will **Luke 1:38.**

The Father's Business:

Jesus obeyed the Father's will even at a young age, as seen when He was found in the temple **Luke 2:49.**

Baptism and Affirmation:

His baptism affirmed His obedience to God's plan
Matthew 3:13-17.

Temptation:

Jesus faced temptation but remained obedient to God's Word *Matthew 4:1-11.*

Submission to God's Will:

Throughout His ministry, Jesus demonstrates obedience to the Father's will *John 5:30.*

Humility in Service:

Jesus exemplified obedience through humble service, washing His disciples' feet *John 13:4-5.*

Suffering and Obedience on the Cross:

Jesus' ultimate act of obedience was demonstrated on the cross *Matthew 26:39.*

Apostle Paul's Example:

Galatians 2:20 reveals Paul's surrendered life, living by faith in Christ. Paul's transformation from a persecutor to an Apostle demonstrates obedience and yieldedness. His endurance through trials in *2 Corinthians 11:23-28* shows his steadfast faith.

Abraham's Obedience.

Abraham's test with Isaac illustrates steadfast faith and readiness to obey.

Job's Surrender:

Job's acceptance of God's will in suffering demonstrates unwavering faith *Job 1:21.*

His resilience and trust in God's sovereignty during trials reveal his surrendered spirit.

God's Apparent Silence:

Obedience and reliance on God's integrity highlighted during divine quiet. Trusting God means surrendering to His plan and will, even in silence.

Moses and David as Examples:

Moses' obedience led Israel through the wilderness despite unclear instructions.

David's surrendered spirit in the Psalms, waiting on the Lord's timing *Psalm 27:14.*

God's Covenant of Obedience:

Emphasises a lifestyle of obedience and yieldedness before, during, and after quiet seasons.

Questioning if one is willing to follow God's instructions, no matter the circumstances.

Trust in God's Plans:

Encourages trust in God's plans, surpassing immediate understanding. Yielding with the knowledge that God rules over human affairs.

Hope in Obedience:

Testimonies of hope in obedience that goes beyond audible instructions: Relying on yielded hearts and unwavering trust, especially in God's apparent silence.

Endurance and Patience:

Demonstrations of enduring obedience, even in the face of trials: Patience and waiting on the Lord's timing as a posture of obedience.

Moses and David as Role Models:

Moses and David exemplify obedience and yieldedness, even without clear instructions.

True Obedience Beyond Audible:

True obedience relies on yielded hearts and unwavering trust, especially when God's voice seems distant.

Chapter 10

The Aftermath of God's Silence

The heart of God's silence deeply resonates with the human experience, providing spiritual transformation and personal development amongst many others. emerging much stronger and resolute. Referencing the moulting period of the eagle as an illustrative example, we see individuals and corporate entities experience seasons of resilience and renewal, emerging much stronger and resolute.

The analogy of the eagle's moulting period beautifully mirrors the human experience of God's silence. Just as the eagle undergoes a season of renewal and transformation, individuals and communities also go through periods of resilience and personal development during times of divine quietness.

Similar to the eagle shedding its old feathers, God's silence often prompts individuals to let go of old mindsets, habits, and ways of living that no longer serve them. This process of shedding enables them to emerge stronger, more resilient, and spiritually transformed, ready to face the challenges and opportunities ahead.

During these silent seasons, individuals may experience significant transitions and growth, much like the eagle navigating the skies and surveying the landscape with its keen vision. This period of introspection and renewal prepares them to soar to new heights and embrace their divine purpose with clarity and confidence.

Just as the eagle's moulting period is essential for its continued strength and vitality, so too is God's silence a crucial aspect of the believer's spiritual journey. It is during these silent seasons that individuals have the opportunity to deepen their faith, cultivate resilience, and experience personal growth, ultimately emerging as stronger and more purposeful followers of Christ.

Throughout the process, the eagle's innate abilities remain intact, despite the temporary vulnerabilities. The feathers, symbolic of strength and prowess, are renewed, ensuring optimal flight and protection. The powerful talons, vital for hunting and survival, also undergo a process of renewal, reinforcing its capacity to seize opportunities and overcome obstacles.

Individuals find inspiration in the eagle's process of renewal and transformation. Embracing their own period of silence and change, similar to the eagle, can lead to growth and a deeper connection with faith and purpose. As the eagle emerges from its silent season, ready for adventurous flights, individuals, families, corporate bodies, and nations can emerge from their own God's silent moments transformed and renewed, prepared to embrace challenges and opportunities that await.

During the moulting phase that spans approximately 150 days, the eagle undergoes a transformative process, shedding its old feathers enduring physical discomfort.

This period can be compared to a silent season marked by uncertainties, challenges and vulnerabilities. But in the face of the struggle, the eagle finds encouragement and support from other eagles who have been through the experience making sounds of flight and dropping pieces of meat in the valley occasionally. During the process, some eagles falter, unable to withstand, while others exhibit resilience and determination and eventually emerging stronger.

As the moulting eagle ascends the valley, embarking on its transformative experience, it locates a rock for the purpose of removing the calcium mass encasing its beak by painfully hitting it to a rock, bleeds and awaits healing.

The next is to remove the weak talons using the new beak, allowing them to heal, and finally, sheds the feathers using its beak, bathes in the sun to release oil to promote the growth of fresh ones. The eagle readies itself for a new phase of adventure, exemplifying a renewed strength.

Ready for the next 30 or more years of its life span, the eagle takes to the skies in the midst of storm currents. Reflecting the process, from the depths of the valley to the heights of the sky, mirroring the nature of life's challenges and its rewards. Just as the eagle emerges from its moulting phase revitalised and renewed, individuals too can discover strength and purpose in adversity on the strength of God's guidance.

Rewards of the Aftermath

Feather Renewal:

Moulting is crucial for eagles to replace damaged or worn-out feathers, which are vital for flight, insulation, and protection. Healthy feathers ensure the eagle's ability to soar, hunt effectively, and survive in the wild.

Life Stage Significance:

The timing of moulting varies with the eagle's age and life stage. Juvenile eagles experience their first moult within the first year, transitioning from immature to distinctive adult plumage. Adult eagles molt annually, usually after the breeding season, marking significant stages of life.

Temporary Vulnerability:

During moulting, eagles face temporary vulnerability as they shed old feathers and await the growth of new ones. This period can limit their ability to fly, emphasising the need for secure perches and avoidance of potential threats for safety and survival.

Symbolism and significance:

The moulting process holds symbolic significance, representing renewal, transformation, and growth. Eagles, symbolic of strength and freedom, provide significance of spiritual renewal. Shedding old feathers symbolism letting go of the past, while new feather growth signifies fresh and new beginnings.

Conservation and Observation:

Observing moulting eagles provides opportunities for wildlife enthusiasts and researchers to study these majestic birds up close. Monitoring the eagles population during moulting seasons contribute to conservation efforts aimed at protecting these iconic species and their habitats.

Adaptations for Survival:

Moulting is an adaptive strategy for the eagle's survival, it ensures they maintain optimal flight capabilities, which is so crucial for hunting and avoiding predators. Constant feather renewal enhances their survival in the wild as apex predators. Overall, the moulting season is a natural and essential aspect of the eagle's life cycle, enhancing their physical capabilities, adaptation to the environment, and a symbol of renewal and transformation. Embracing the challenges of moulting is vital for survival and flourishing, highlighting the importance of change and growth in one life's journey.

Biblical Perspectives.

Unveiling the Outcomes of God's Silence.

Spiritual Growth and Insight:

Seasons of divine silence often lead to a deep spiritual growth and insight. Figures like Job and the Psalmists emerged from such periods with a deeper understanding of God's sovereignty, faith and self-awareness. Their experiences serve as testaments of transformation having endured silent seasons in one's spiritual journey.

Preparation for a Greater Calling:

Biblical players like Joseph and David experienced the season of God's silence or obscurity before assuming significant roles. These moments of God's silence served as a preparatory window for individuals destined for greater callings. Their experiences highlight how silence can be a prelude to God's intervention and the fulfilment of God's plans.

Cultivating Patience and Perseverance:

Virtues of patience and perseverance finds a fertile ground in the window of God's silence. Examples like Abraham's patient wait for a promised son illustrate the cultivation of these qualities during silent seasons.

Restoration and Redemption Purposes:

The biblical account of the Egyptian bondage and the exile in Babylon helps to illustrate how God's silence can serve as John the Baptist' to usher in seasons of restoration and redemption. This season led to a dramatic intervention of God, resulting in miraculous signs, emancipation, and the fulfilment of His promises.

God's silence, therefore, is a call to a transformative phase leading to redemptive actions, emphasising God's faithfulness and sovereignty.

Prophetic Revelation:

God's silence often precedes prophetic revelation and divine guidance. Prophets like Isaiah and Jeremiah received messages of hope and restoration after periods of perceived silence and discipline. These revelations offer guidance and reassurance to individuals walking through silent seasons, pointing towards a future of hope and restoration.

Transformation and Renewal:

God's silence contributes to personal and collective transformation. Individuals and communities undergo renewal, turning back to God with a renewed commitment and understanding after moments of silence. These experiences highlight the transformative nature of divine encounters and the restoration that follows the period.

Strengthened Faith and Trust:

Those who encounter God's silence emerge with their faith strengthened. Consider the journey of Abraham to sacrifice Isaac, a powerful example of how moments of silence deepen our trust in God's providence. Through trials and challenges, our faith endures, leading to a deeper connection with God.

In closing, these dimensions of God's silence illuminate the varied ways in which He works during silent seasons. The narratives from Scripture serve as a testament to, test and refine our faith, showing how reliance on God perseveres through diverse challenges and trials, ultimately resulting in spiritual growth, renewal, and redemption.

Contemporary Perspective.

Encountering God's silence can leave one deeply impacted, both positively and negatively. These explains why.

Positive Responses.

Growth and Inner Tenacity:

God's silence builds in people growth and resilience, making one wiser and stronger.

Resetting Priorities:

One may want to reassess their objectives and values in life, seeking a more meaningful existence after going through periods of God's silence.

Renewed Relationships:

It can positively impact and refine relationships, building trust, understanding, and care.

Social Awareness:

It can inspire social awareness and environmental concerns, motivating individuals to contribute positively to society and be a blessing to humanity.

As Part of God's program in Life's Journey:

It may lead us to understand that the divine pause is a part of God's program for life's journey on earth.

The Search for Understanding:

Many people seek meaning to the significance the silence holds.

Resilience and Perseverance:

It can lead to cultivating resilience and perseverance, strengthening individuals' faith to withstand challenges.

Appreciating God's Wisdom:

When individuals experience moments of God's silence and understand its purpose and meaning. They may come to appreciate that the pause is not without reason, but are part of God's program for their lives. This understanding invites a sense of comfort and trust, knowing that God's wisdom guides every aspect of their journey on earth.

Negative Responses.

The Feeling of Abandonment:

During times of adversity or crisis, the purposeful withholding of God's voice and intervention may foster feelings of abandonment, leading to questioning His omnipresence, omnipotence, omniscience and omnibenevolence.

Questioning God's Plan:

When prayers, fasting, offerings etc seem to go unanswered and situations do not improve, one may begin to doubt God's plan for their lives, wondering if there is a purpose behind the challenges they are dealing with.

Struggling with Faith:

The absence of clear signs from God can foster doubts about one's faith, leading to questioning the existence of God or the validity of one's faith.

Emotional Disturbance:

The silence of God can cause frustration, anger and despair, as individuals grapple with seasons of apparent divine no show.

Seeking Clarity:

In times of uncertainty, people may question the process of God's silence, wondering why He is saying nothing on matters of importance or situations in their lives.

Facing Unanswered Prayers:

Persistent prayers without tangible proofs can indeed lead to doubts, questioning the very foundation of prayer, and asking if God truly hears and responds to one's petitions. When we pray earnestly for something, especially when facing challenges or seeking solutions to our problems, we naturally hope to see visible results or tangible evidence of God's intervention.

Struggling with Identity:

In the silence of God, individuals may foster questions about their identity and purpose, wondering if they are truly valued and loved by their Creator.

Coping with Loss:

During times of loss and grief, the silence of God may intensify feelings of sorrow and confusion, as individuals seek comfort and understanding.

Challenges to Trust:

The prolonged silence of God can be challenging to one's trust in His promises and faithfulness, leading to doubting if God can truly be relied on in difficult times.

Losing Faith in God and Withdrawing from Church:

Some people, in response to God's silence, change their view of God or even question His existence. Whilst others distance themselves from the church, feeling frustrated and disappointed.

Despair and the Struggle for Survival:

In the depths of God's silence, some grapple with the feelings of despair, leading to thoughts of self-harm or suicidal tendencies as they struggle to cope with overwhelming emotions.

These responses unfold the impact on individuals and the importance of support from matured, godly leaders, counsellors, and communities going through silent seasons. Additionally, reflections on thinkers like Elie Wiesel and Richard Rubenstein, referencing their negative view of God after the Holocaust, offer insights into how some people grapple with faith and God's silence in the face of adversity.

Highlights.

Symbolism of the Eagle:

The eagle symbolises strength, majesty, and unique qualities that demand admiration.

Impressive Lifespan:

The eagle can live for 70 years or more, navigating the skies with keen vision.

Silent Season of Renewal:

The first 40 years of an eagle's life represent a silent season marked by growth and transition.

Renewed Strength:

Shedding old feathers and undergoing physical changes makes the eagle stronger and more resilient.

Inherent Abilities Intact:

Despite vulnerability, the eagle's strength and prowess are renewed for optimal flight and protection.

Inspiration for Growth:

Individuals find inspiration in the eagle's process of renewal and transformation.

Embracing The Change:

Similar to the eagle, embracing periods of silence and change leads to growth and deeper faith.

Preparation for Challenges:

Emerging from silent seasons, individuals are prepared to confront challenges and opportunities.

Transformative Experience:

The moulting phase, lasting about 150 days, is transformative, comparable to divine silence.

Resilience and Determination:

Some eagles falter, while others exhibit resilience and determination, emerging stronger.

Process of Renewal:

The eagle meticulously removes old beak encasings, weak talons, and old feathers for renewal.

Ready for Adventure:

After the moulting phase, the eagle is prepared for the next 30 years of life, ready to soar.

Journey of Strength:

From the depths of the valley to the heights of the sky, mirroring life's challenges and rewards.

Symbolic Significance:

The moulting process symbolises renewal, transformation, and growth for individuals.

Embracing Challenges:

Embracing the challenges of silent seasons is vital for spiritual growth, resilience, and purpose.

Epilogue:

God's silence is a significant and purposeful pause within His sovereign plan. It is not an absence but a defining and transformative interval. Embracing this moment allows individuals, families and nations to align with His sovereign will, where his subtle voice refines and prepares them for the next phase of His evolving agenda.

Intentional Design:

It explains that God's silence is not random but purposefully designed. Just as a composer strategically places rests in music to enhance its beauty, God orchestrates moments of silence to amplify the impact of His divine work in our lives.

A Test of Faith:

It suggests that during the periods of divine silence, our faith undergoes a refining process similar to gold in a fire. It acknowledges the natural inclination to question and doubt, yet encourages us to anchor our faith in the unchanging truth of God's promises.

Hope in His Silence:

Rather than succumbing to despair, God's silence is a call to look ahead with unwavering hope. It serves as a reminder that our experience is still unfolding, and God, as the Author of Life, is crafting a masterpiece beyond our imagination.

Growing in Faith:

Similar to the eagle rising above storm clouds, we're urged to rise above the challenges of God's silence with wings of faith. This stretching of faith leads to greater intimacy with our Creator.

Embracing Unconditional Love:

At the core of God's silence is His unconditional love. This love remains constant and unwavering, even when the world around us falls still. In the embrace of His love, we discover the strength to endure, the courage to hope, and the faith to believe that He is working all things together for our good.

Trusting in His Timing:

God's silence beckons us to trust in His perfect timing. Just as a seed lies dormant in the soil beneath before bursting forth into new life, we are being prepared in the quiet of His presence for the season of fruitfulness ahead.

Seeking His Presence:

Rather than filling the silence with noise and distractions, it calls us to seek the stillness of God's presence. In this quiet, we can access His gentle voice showing the way towards righteousness and peace.

Resting in His Promises:

During moments of doubt and despair, we find rest in God's unshakeable promises. illuminating our path through the darkest of moments.

A Season of Preparation:

God's silence often precedes new beginnings and fresh revelations. It's a time to discard old ways, making room for the new work God wants to do in our lives.

Renewed Strength and Resilience:

Like an eagle moulting old feathers, we're stripped of the old to become stronger and ready for new heights.

Discovering Hidden Treasures:

In the depth of God's silence, there are hidden treasures waiting for those who dare to explore. This quest leads to uncovering the gems of His truth, love, and grace.

A Call to Surrender:

Ultimately, God's silence is a call to surrender our plans to His sovereign will. In this surrender, we find true peace, joy, and fulfilment.

Finally Brethren:.

In the symphony of God's silence, may we find the courage to listen, the strength to endure, and the faith to believe that God is indeed at work in ways unseen. As we navigate the uncharted waters of His silence, may we emerge on the other side, transformed, renewed, and overflowing with the love and grace of our Heavenly Father.

So, let's embrace this divine pause, this holy hush, with open hearts and willing spirits. For in His silence, one discovers the beauty of His ever-presence, the depth of God's love, and the certainty of His promises. Although the journey may be long and the path uncertain, we walk it with confidence, knowing that one is never alone, for He who promised is faithful.

Let's journey together, hand in hand with the One who walks beside us in silence, guiding us with His wisdom, sustaining us with His grace, and leading us ever closer to the fullness of His purpose for our lives in Jesus mighty Name. Amen.

About the Book

Unveiling the Mysteries of God's Silence is a compelling walk of destiny into the Significant relationship between God and humanity. This captivating book sheds light on the intricacies of God's quietude, providing invaluable insights to navigate the complexities of faith.
Unpacking the Voice of God: Embark on a deep exploration of the diverse ways God speaks to us. Peer into "The Deep Voice of God's Silence," unravelling the spiritual significance of moments when God's voice seems veiled or distant. God Breaks the Silence: Experience transformative moments where divine revelations pierce through the quietude, revealing deep truths. Contemplate "The Purpose of God's Silence," understanding God's intentions behind these silent seasons.

Biblical Players: Traverse alongside biblical figures whose encounters with God's silence and revelation shape the course of history. Discover lessons from their narratives of resilience, devoted faith, and transformation. The Significance of God's Silence: shedding more light on the transformative power of silent seasons as refining fires that purify our faith and draw us closer to God's heart. Obedience and Yieldedness to God's Will: Emphasising the importance of vulnerability and surrender in silence, urging readers to embrace these virtues as pathways to spiritual growth.

The Aftermath of God's Silence: Discover that silent seasons are not voids to be feared but spheres of encounter, where faith is renewed, understanding deepens, and the presence of God is keenly felt. Each chapter offers captivating exploration of the God-human relationship, providing guidance and wisdom for those navigating the depths of faith. "Unveiling the Mysteries of God's Silence" is not just a book, but a transformative destiny walk through the realms of faith.

We want to hear from You.

If this book has impacted or inspired you in any way, please share your story with us. Your testimony has the power to encourage others in their spiritual journey.

Whether a particular passage spoke to your heart, a prayer connected with you deeply, or you felt closer to God through quiet reflection as you read, we would love to hear how this book blessed you.

Please take a few minutes to write out your testimony and email it to **testimony@pneumalife.com** or visit our website at www.pneumalife.com/testimony to share your experience.

Your story matters - it helps spread the transformative message of God's love and grace. Thank you for partnering with us on this journey of faith. May you continue to feel God's presence guiding your path today and always.

With gratitude,
Pneuma Life Publishing

UNVEILING THE MYSTERIES OF
GOD'S SILENCE

Samuel Sowah, an Apostle of Jesus Christ to the nations, with three decades of experience preaching the gospel of the everlasting kingdom of God across four continents and more than ten African Nations. Dr. Sowah is a dynamic preacher, a sought-after conference speaker, a prolific writer and author, and a mentor to many. Samuel Sowah has held various leadership roles, including serving as the African coordinator for Igreja da Communhao Agape - Brasil, Latin America.

He also served as the CEO of Weep Not Africa Mission, an NGO dedicated to humanitarian activities, demonstrating his commitment to making a positive impact. Additionally, he acted as the Ghana Coordinator for the International Gathering of Eagles Canada and served as the President at Guccad Ghana, an international Christian body for Africans in the diaspora. He also held the role of coordinator for the Guccad Presidents in Africa.

Samuel Sowah currently serves as the visionary and Chief Servant over Kingdom Action Ministries International and The Apostolic Gathering. He is an active executive member of the network of Intercessors of Ghana. Dr. Sowah holds an honorary Doctor of Divinity degree from Prixton Church & University, CA, USA, and a Doctor of Leadership and Humanity degree from St.Thomas-a-Becket University Institute, Africa Campus. He is married and blessed with children.

www.ingramcontent.com/pod-product-compliance
Lightning Source LLC
Chambersburg PA
CBHW051127160426
43195CB00014B/2380